6·7·72.

AUTHOR	CLASS No.
ELLIOT, C.	629.1309
TITLE	BOOK No.
AERONAUTS AND AVIATORS.	77206984

AERONAUTS AND AVIATORS

AERONAUTS AND AVIATORS

An account of man's endeavours in the air over Norfolk, Suffolk and East
Cambridgeshire between 1785 and 1939

by

CHRISTOPHER ELLIOTT

Foreword by Sir ALAN COBHAM, K.B.E., A.F.C., Hon.F.R.Ae.S

TERENCE DALTON LIMITED

LAVENHAM   SUFFOLK

1971

Published by
TERENCE DALTON LIMITED
S B N 900963 21 2

Printed in Great Britain at

THE LAVENHAM PRESS LIMITED
LAVENHAM   SUFFOLK

Dedicated to the Stone Age of Flying when, above all else, initiative and good comradeship were essential—indeed, were often the only means of survival.

CONTENTS

INDEX OF ILLUSTRATIONS

ACKNOWLEDGEMENTS

A work such as this must depend a great deal on original and published sources. First and foremost I owe thanks to the respective editors of the *Bury Free Press,* the *Cambridge Evening News,* the *East Anglian Daily Times,* the *East Anglian Magazine,* the *Eastern Daily Press,* the *Norwich Mercury Series* and the *Suffolk Mercury Series* for the help they have given me over the past 20 years by publishing articles and letters which have revived memories and caused people—particularly those belonging to the Stone Age of Flying—to commit vital details to paper.

Then I must acknowledge those people who have given me special help. I must thank Mrs. C. Anne Hammond, of Aldringham, for talking about Orfordness and Martlesham Heath in World War I, and for allowing me to take away for copying her late husband's most precious photo albums; Mrs. Gladys Carr, of Hendon, for more information on Martlesham Heath and her husband, the late Reginald Carr, who started his flying career as mechanic to Claude Grahame-White; Mr. Eugene C. M. Prentice, of Harkstead, and his mother, Mrs Joy Courtney Prentice, of Menton, France, for an insight into the early days of flying in Suffolk and at Hendon; Captain A. A. Rice, of Cringleford, for helpful guidance over the early days of flying at Norwich; Mr. D. J. Paul, of Boulton and Paul Ltd., Norwich, for his courtesy in turning up information about local World War I aircraft production. Mr. Eugene C. Ulph, of Beccles, for his memories of the early flying experiments at Beccles; Miss Betty Woods, of Tring, and the Woods family generally for freely allowing use of notes left by the late Captain Harry W. Woods; Mr. Harald Penrose, of Sherborne, for talking about the day he escaped from the P.V.7 near Wickham Market; Mr. George Swain, of Norwich, pioneer local photographer, for turning up long forgotten photographs of aeroplanes and airships; Mr. H. Carrington, of Caister, for his memories of Sedgeford; Mr. Gordon Kinsey, of Ipswich, for advice on Martlesham Heath about which he has compiled a major work; Miss F. Barton, Sir Alan Cobham's secretary, for checking on Sir Alan's visits to East Anglia in the early days; Mrs. Doreen Rope, of Kesgrave, for providing details about the local R.101 memorial; Mr. W. C. H. Hubbard, of Pulham St. Mary, for rare airship pictures; Mrs. Ivy Woollard, of Felixstowe, for memories of the early seaplane days; Mr. Donald Parker, of Barton Mills, for details about his famous brother, John Lankester Parker; Air Marshal Sir Arthur Longmore, of Sunningdale, for guidance on the air operations near Thetford in 1912; Mr. Whitney Straight of Southall, for making available papers about the development of Ipswich airport; Lady Margery Quilter of Woodbridge, for photographs of the late Sir Raymond Quilter, the Suffolk parachute expert; Lady Cayley, of Brompton-by-Sawdon, for confirming the Norwich link with Sir George Cayley, inventor of the modern aeroplane; Mr. C. R. Temple, of Norwich, for turning out many of his own rare photographs of early aviation events; Mrs. Alice M. Tomlinson, of Lowestoft, for permission to publish her late husband's poem, 'Vapour Trail'; Mr. Trevor Jones, Jesus College

Cambridge Society, for details of the 18th century balloonist Edward D. Clarke; Mr. Philip Jarrett, of the Royal Aeronautical Society, for assistance; Mr. M. A. Smith, of Benhall Green, for memories of Bircham Newton in 1939; Mr. M. P. Sayer, of Chinnor, for information about J. E. Humphreys, the Wivenhoe air pioneer; Dr. P. J. Hynes, of London, S.W.18, for help over Zeppelin activity in World War I; Mr. C. F. Morris, of Hatfield, for photographs, including those of the Sanders biplane at Beccles; Mr. Derek Wood, author of *The Narrow Margin,* for photographs of the early days of radar in Suffolk; Lord Trenchard, of North Mymms, for the photograph of his father, founder of the R.A.F., believed taken near Thetford in 1912; Mr. Charles L. Elliott, of Earley, nr. Reading, for information about Pulham and other East Anglian aviation happenings; Mrs. L. H. Sheppard, of Felixstowe, for the loan of scarce copies of *The Wing* and *Pulham Patrol;* Mr. Frank Hussey, of Ipswich, for guidance on Felixstowe matters; Mr. W. Cross, of Felixstowe, for rare pictures of Winston Churchill's seaplane at Clacton; Miss Rosemary Risk, of Sudbury, whose father, Wing Commander C. E. Risk, was first C.O., for press cuttings about flying events at Felixstowe; Mr. C. H. Kimber, of Metfield, for more Pulham memories; Mr. A. J. Orange, of Feltwell, for local airfield developments between the wars; Mr. A. A. C. Jordan, of Aylsham, for facts about World War I aircraft production by Mann Egerton & Co. Ltd., Norwich; Mr. Frank Tonkinson, of Ipswich, for details of sale of early aeronautical prints and drawings; Mr. Henry Clarke, of Ipswich, for suggestions on the whereabouts of early photographs; Mr. R. Forbes-Morgan, of Streatham, S.W.16., for help over Lawrence of Arabia at Felixstowe; Mr. A. Mattinson, of Saxmundham, for memories of early aviation incidents in Norfolk; Mr. Robert Malster, of Ipswich, for details of a violent aeroplane crash near Norwich in 1916; Air Marshal Sir Robert Saundby, of Burghclere, for giving me a first hand account of the end of the L.48; Mr. E. C. Hine and Mr. G. Pleasance, of the Imperial War Museum, for help with pictures.

In addition I have to acknowledge the following people and organisations: Mr. S. J. Cox (Airways Union Ltd.), Mr. Allan Jobson, Mr. H. E. Fleetwood (Group Publicity Manager, Boulton & Paul Ltd.), Mr. Ian McLachlan, Mr. G. B. Dick, Mr. W. C. Bell (Publicity Department, Ransomes Sims & Jefferies Ltd.), Mr. Bruce Robertson, Mr. Owen Thetford, Mr. Peter Corbell, Flight Lieutenant Keith Answell (R.A.F. Wattisham), Miss Ann C. Tilbury (*Flight International*), Mr. A. J. Jackson, Mr. M. J. F. Bowyer, Mr. H. S. Sawyer, Captain R. N. Phillips, Mr. G. F. Cordy, Mr. Donald Black, Mr. Jack Easedown, Mr. Donald Smith, Mr. D. J. Proctor (Norfolk & Norwich Aero Club Ltd.), Mr. R. G. Francis (Marshall of Cambridge (Engineering) Ltd.),. Squadron Leader H. J. Brown (retd.), Dr. I. Granger, Mr. A. W. Naylor (Royal Aeronautical Society), Flight Lieutenant P. B. Hadlington (R.A.F. Marham), Mrs. M. Drake, Mr. S. W. Slaughter, Miss R. Young (Bridewell Museum, Norwich), Mr. P. Webb (Deputy Personnel Manager, Richard Garrett Engineering Works Ltd.), Mrs. G. E. Sage (former honorary secretary of the Crabbe Memorial Competition), Mr. R. E. W. Chatters, Miss H. Clapham, and others who in chance conversations over the years led me to new material.

Air Historical Branch, Ministry of Defence; The Felixstowe Dock & Railway Company, Norfolk and Norwich Record Office, Moyse's Hall Museum, The Royal Aeronautical Society, University of Reading Museum of English Rural Life, Abbot's Hall Museum of Rural Life of East Anglia, Ipswich & Suffolk East Record Office, Imperial War Museum, Great Yarmouth Port & Haven Commissioners, Great Yarmouth Central Library, East Suffolk County Council, The Feltwell Historical & Archaeological Society, Ipswich Reference Library, Borough of Beccles, Merton Public Libraries, City of Westminster Public Libraries, Cambridgeshire and Isle of Ely Record Office.

However, having made use of so many sources I alone am responsible for the presentation of the information which was so freely given. Last but not least I have to thank Mr. John Venmore-Rowland, the General Editor for Terence Dalton Ltd., for quiet encouragement; and my wife Elizabeth for chasing up material and pictures on my behalf—a long process gladly delegated to her.

Christopher Elliott
Wimbledon
1971

Someone takes a brush and paints a line
Straight as a dagger through the empty sky,
Someone pours a flask of smoking wine
Down from the tables of the gods on high,
And a vapour trail from a plane on the climb
Is born in heaven in the evening light,
Joining today to the rest of time
Like a song in the sky to the age of flight;
High in its own eternity,
Hand over hand it climbs up the world,
Climbing as high as the world can be,
Then rolls from the sky like an ensign furled;
Then someone takes a tin of scarlet dye
And spills a sunset on the emptied sky!

—'Vapour Trail' from *The Waveney Sonnets* by the late A. E. Tomlinson, the Lowestoft poet, who was the first winner of the Crabbe Memorial poetry competition organised by the Suffolk Poetry Society in 1954.

FOREWORD

by

Sir ALAN J. COBHAM, K.B.E., A.F.C., Hon.F.R.Ae.S.

EAST ANGLIA is a brave country—Norfolk, Suffolk and Essex have stood the brunt of two World Wars. Their beautiful countryside and rich farmland has been desecrated by a mass of wartime aerodromes. The farming community suffered the agony of having their wonderful agricultural land requisitioned at a moment's notice by the Government for Service Aerodromes and I suppose there are still miles of concrete runways which have never been reclaimed.

I started going to Saxham near Bury St. Edmunds at the age of five; then it was gorgeous rural country and my memories of fishing in ponds and lakes, of hanging around the blacksmith's forge and watching Shire horses being shod and of wandering through the woods are all very vivid.

One bright autumn day in 1918 when I was an instructor in the Flying Corps at Manston it was my duty to lead my flight on a cross country journey to our new home, Narborough in Norfolk, where I was to spend two or three months of intensive instruction amid charming local inhabitants who were so hospitable and my memories of East Dereham, Downham Market, King's Lynn and Swaffham are amongst my happiest recollections.

During the last war I visited so many of the aerodromes in connection with special equipment my company was supplying to the Air Force Squadrons and now today the home of flight refuelling for the Royal Air Force is at Marham in Norfolk. My visits to Marham always bring back happy memories of the days when I was an instructor at Narborough for, curiously, my flight hangar of 1919 is still standing—or at least part of it—on the far corner of Marham Aerodrome.

East Anglia has played an important part in the history of British Aviation and we must thank Christopher Elliott for all his research work, so necessary in compiling the glorious record of all that these Eastern counties have done for British Aviation.

Tortola,
British Virgin Islands.
1971

INTRODUCTION

When people learnt that I was researching for a two volume study covering the growth of aviation in East Anglia, beginning with the early balloon ascents from Norwich in the 1780s, some expressed surprise, doubting that there was enough early evidence in such a small area of man's endeavours in the air. Others declared that Essex could not be excluded from East Anglia. Their doubts, I am pleased to say, were confounded by the amount of evidence which turned up from many written and original sources. Moreover, there are good grounds for claiming that East Anglia—Norfolk, Suffolk and east Cambridgeshire—stands out, as much as any other part of the country, Farnborough included, as the great testing area for all kinds of aerial contraptions over some 180 years. Why is this? Well, airmen, who should know, tell me that the reason is simple: the flat, inviting countryside. Another factor is that, being the nearest point to Germany, East Anglia attracted in the 20th century air stations which in later years expanded into test centres.

Try to imagine all the movements of airborne bodies in the East Anglian sky since the first balloon ascents from Norwich in the 1780s. Including the two world wars, when Zeppelins criss-crossed the area by night and V-2 rockets—forerunners of the moon rockets—crashed without warning on Norfolk in the middle 1940s, the sky would be so full of shapes by day and lights by night that the prophet Ezekiel could truthfully claim: 'I told you so'.

Think, too, of the many dangerous situations which must have arisen in the area during that time—the aeronaut Money drifting out to sea in a balloon with a jammed release valve . . . Zeppelin crew members, to avoid being incinerated, leaping without parachutes over Suffolk by night . . . test pilot Penrose, having lost a wing, making the first ever escape in Britain from an enclosed cockpit near Wickham Market . . . the airship men fighting to bring back the crippled R33 to Pulham . . . the physical suffering of World War I aviators who, with little if any survival gear, were prepared to freeze in open cockpits as they chugged after Zeppelins and Gothas over the North Sea to the point of no return. These were individualists of a kind never to be seen again in the air. Our proud and only consolation so long afterwards is that at least they performed some of their epics —and quite a few antics—over and around East Anglia.

But first a word about the beginnings of man's endeavours in the air—the events which led up to the first balloon ascents from Norwich in the 1780s.

From the earliest periods of history man predicted flight. For example, the prophet Ezekiel did in 595 B.C., and some quotations from his Old Testament writings were embodied in a postcard published early this century. However, it was Leonardo da Vinci (1452-1519), the Italian painter and sculptor, in about 1500 who was the first man scientifically to consider flying. Among his designs was one for a flapping wing aircraft—an ornithopter—but it led nowhere. His work remained unknown until late Victorian times, so he never even inspired other inventors.

Many people believe that the aeroplane started with the Wright Brothers. The truth of the matter is that the real inventor of the modern aeroplane was a talented Yorkshire baronet named Sir George Cayley, whose great great granddaughter learnt to fly at Norwich in the 1920s. Between 1799 and 1810, Cayley not only laid the foundations of the science of aerodynamics, but made successful model gliders to demonstrate his theories in practice. Furthermore, Cayley finally built and flew—with his coachman as the guinea pig—the first man-carrying glider of history in 1852-1853. This machine with inherent lateral longitudinal stability, adjustable fin and tailplane, nacelle with tricycle undercarriage, and pilot operated controls, incorporated the basic features of the modern aeroplane. So much for Cayley's glider. What led East Anglia to take an interest in balloons?

It was the Montgolfier brothers, Joseph and Etienne, of France, who translated into reality the centuries' old dream of flight. These brothers, as a prelude to human flight, decided to discover whether animals, unaccustomed to the rarefied atmosphere, would be injured at the heights attainable by their balloons. So on September 19, 1783, a Montgolfier balloon was sent up from Versailles with three living occupants in its wicker basket—a duck, a cock and a sheep. Their eight minute voyage took them a distance of one and a half miles. Only damage sustained by the 'crew' was a slight injury to the wing of the cock, 'such as might have been accounted for by a kick from the sheep'.

On November 21, 1783, J. F. Pilâtre de Rozier and a companion, the Marquis d'Arlandes, at a little before 2 p.m., went up in a free balloon and in 25 minutes travelled at between 300 and 500 feet on a five and a half mile journey across Paris. The two aeronauts landed safely and, as their balloon settled on the ground, the conquest of the air by Man had begun.

From then on interest in ballooning spread all over Europe, creating a sensation in learned and scientific circles. Following the achievement of the Montgolfier brothers, balloon ascents were made in the British Isles, the first from English soil being by Vincent Lunardi on September 15, 1784, from Moorfields, London, to Hertfordshire. Norwich, as far as records show, undoubtedly witnessed—in 1785—the first flight of an aeronaut in East Anglia and this, in fact, is where our story starts . . . .

NOTE: As the R.A.F. was the child of the Army and the Navy, and mixed Service ranks were freely used in World War I, in most cases in the book the ranks applicable at the time are used unless otherwise indicated.

H. M. King George V and his sons The Prince of Wales (King Edward VIII) and the Duke of York (King George VI) at the grand review of the R.A.F. at Mildenhall in 1935.   *R. E. W. Chatters*

CHAPTER I

Ballooning Days

IT WAS at Norwich in 1785 that the air age got off the ground in East Anglia with two or three spectacular balloon flights. First to draw big crowds was James Deeker, tradesman, who sold experimental balloons at 59 Berwick Street, Soho, London, at prices ranging from five shillings for one 3 ft. in diameter 'neatly gilt' (gas threepence) to two guineas for one 12 ft. in diameter (gas five shillings).

Deeker, who was a very clever and ingenious mechanic, attracted much attention at Norwich on June 1, 1785, when it was announced that he was going to make a balloon ascent from Quantrell's Gardens with a 14 year old girl named Weller. Just before 4 o'clock in the afternoon, however, a violent storm tore the lower part of the balloon and some gas escaped through the envelope. The damaged envelope was drawn together and secured with strong cord. Yet another burst of storm, accompanied by lightning, did further damage to the balloon and the lift of 458 lb. was reduced to 300 lb. The girl Weller then climbed back into the balloon car but had to be put out. Now Deeker was on his own and, with the girl gone the balloon went up in an 'almost perpendicular ascent'. However, the rent in the fabric increased to such an extent that it seemed, in Deeker's words, 'large enough to admit a post-chaise'. A rapid fall then followed, for the aeronaut had little ballast left from his fast rising. By hanging to the hoop, Deeker escaped injury on landing at Sisland near Loddon, some 10 miles from Norwich.

Our resolute aeronaut carried out a second ascent from Norwich on June 23, 1785. A high wind again upset his plans and the girl Weller for a second time was disappointed. Deeker lifted off from Quantrell's Gardens, despite the weather, but struck some trees. Then the balloon rose sharply. The normal, though on this occasion somewhat rapid, series of 'ascensions and falls' prevented him from making accurate observations owing to the irregular movements of the balloon's barometer. After a flight of three quarters of an hour Deeker, the man who sold toy balloons in Soho, came down at Topcroft, about 12 miles from Norwich, some horsemen who had followed him helping him to secure the balloon.

What led James Deeker to get himself tied up with a 14 year old girl in two attempts to go aloft? Perhaps he was simply doing what was fashionable. For a month earlier—on May 3—Mlle. Simonet, then only 14½ years old, had accompanied Jean Pierre Blanchard, the French balloonist, on one of his early balloon flights from his Balloon and Parachute Aerostatic Academy off Stockwell Road, Vauxhall, London. This was the first flight by a woman from English soil.

However, Norwich experienced its most exciting balloon spectacle a month later —on July 23, 1785—when Major (later General) John Money* became one of the

*The Royal Aeronautical Society, London, holds a number of publications by Money. In 1799 he wrote *A Partial Re-Organization of the British Army*, in 1803 *A Short Treatise on the Use of Balloons and Field Observators in Military Operations*, and in 1805 *Major General Money's Propositions to Field Marshal Marquis Townsend, For A Volunteer Artillery, in Norfolk*.

Major Money in his balloon coming down in the sea on July 23, 1785. From a print by Clarke dated 1785.
East Suffolk Record Office

first aeronauts to be rescued from the sea. Only a month before his Norwich ascent he had made his first balloon ascent from London.

But first a word about Major Money who had the distinction of being the first man in England to consider military aeronautics from the point of view of actual experience. Major Money, who was born in 1752 and died in 1817, began his military career in the Norfolk Militia, and between the time of his joining the regular army in 1762, to his retirement on half pay in 1784, he saw considerable service in various theatres of war.

In later life he took up farming but still returned from time to time to the consideration of current military affairs. In 1806 he addressed a letter on the defence of London against the threatened French invasion to William Windham, who had been Member for Norwich between 1784 and 1802 and with whom Major Money's interest in ballooning formed a mutual tie.

To return to July 23 when it was recorded that about 700 people, whose admission charges went in aid of the Norfolk and Norwich Hospital, assembled to watch Major Money go aloft, 'some inefficiency in the inflation' of the balloon prevented it from carrying more than the aeronaut himself who did not wish to disappoint the waiting crowd. It is clear that Major Money, who had to throw out his greatcoat to gain extra lift, intended to take up Mr. Jonathan Lockwood and Mr. George Blake—the two men he had accompanied on his first balloon flight on June 3, 1785, from London which finally ended eight miles from Maldon, Essex, although Lockwood had left them when the balloon alighted for a short while during the journey. Major Money and Blake, having emptied the balloon, arrived at Colchester* in a post-chaise.

For Major Money's Norwich ascent, the day was very calm, the leaves on the trees in Quantrell's Gardens, from which the ascent was made, scarcely stirred, and the balloon, rising shortly after 4 o'clock in the afternoon, drifted slowly north west, only to be carried south east by an 'improper current' on rising to a higher elevation. For 45 minutes the balloon was kept in sight from Norwich. It drifted by way of Trowse, Framingham, Willingham, Kirby and Surlingham. 'When over Kirby', it was recorded,

*In 1802, M. Andrè Garnerin, who in Paris in 1797 became the first man to make a successful parachute descent from a balloon, came to London and there repeated his act. On June 28, 1802, while in London, he accompanied Captain R. C. Snowden in a balloon, the pair coming down near Colchester. Garnerin's wife Jeanne Genevieé (1779-1847) was, incidentally, the first professional woman aeronaut and also made parachute descents.

This picture of Major Money about to be rescued by a revenue cutter from Harwich became a best seller. *Royal Aeronautical Society*

'two persons at Framingham called loudly to the major with speaking trumpets, and he answered them by waving the flag at that time'. The balloon—Major Money had only intended a short excursion—had become warmed by the sun and was rising. As he approached the coast he tried to valve gas but it was said that a piece of silk had been sewn over the valve during inflation and consequently it would not open. The aeronaut went into cloud over Pakefield at about 5.35 p.m. and, after being in the air for two hours, came down in the sea about 18 to 20 miles from land in the direction of Southwold. Meanwhile boats had put out from Southwold and Lowestoft but, believing the aeronaut drowned, gave up the search.

As darkness fell Major Money found he was in grave peril. 'For fully five melancholy hours did the major remain in this horrid situation'. A Dutch craft was recorded as having shown 'callous indifference' to his plight, but later it was thought that the crew, with good reason, had taken the balloon for a sea monster! Another boat which had chased him from Suffolk for two hours turned back as night came. Bit by bit the balloon got torn by the waves and more and more gas escaped. Major Money was supported by the hoop and cords but his hands became lacerated as he fought to hold on. Eventually the water was up to his chest.

At 11.30 on the night of July 22 he was spotted by the Harwich revenue cutter *Argus,* under Captain William Haggis, but Major Money was in such a weak condition that he had to be lifted out of the water, the balloon also being taken up. The captain received him with 'great humanity'. On being put to bed, after two or three glasses of grog which Major Money said were 'by far more delicious than champagne', he slept soundly. Early next morning, when he was put ashore at Lowestoft, the news of his unexpected recovery 'put the town in an uproar of delight'. Then Major Money took a post-chaise to his home at Crown Point, near Norwich, arriving in the afternoon.

So much for the brave major. Certainly Major Money was a century ahead in his thinking of the military application of ballooning. For the practical development of ballooning in the British Army did not begin until 1878, when authority was given for the experimental production of balloons and field equipment in Woolwich Arsenal. There was an initial grant of £150 for the construction of a balloon. But even if Major Money's dream took a hundred years to find supporters his ducking in the North Sea in 1785 became a celebrated incident to remember. An engraving of a picture by P. Reinagle called 'The Perilous Situation of Major Money'—it showed the major fighting for his life as the balloon all but drew him beneath the waves—was a best seller.

Major Money's interest in ballooning must have been lasting. We know he was watching balloon ascents at Norwich until two years before his death in 1817. For instance, when a Mr. Seward made a balloon ascent in 1815 from Prussia Gardens—Mr. Seward ended up in a garden nearby—the major was watching. In the same year, when a Mr. Sadler went aloft in a balloon from Ranelagh Gardens, as Quantrell's Gardens were then called, Major Money was there to wish him well.

Indeed, it seems as if Norwich, having pioneered the East Anglian sky, was determined to keep the novelty alive. *The Norwich Mercury* for September 26, 1840, reported that 'on Thursday morning it was announced by the bellman that this stupendous machine would take its long looked for flight. . .'. And the machine? Well, it was the Nassau Balloon, which about that time was thought likely to be used in an attempt to cross the Atlantic. On September 24 in a meadow by the river near Bishopgate bridge, Norwich, Mr. Charles Green* (1785-1870), the son of a London fruiterer, ascended with six passengers. The towers and steeples of the cathedral and all the churches were, it was reported, filled with spectators.

Elsewhere there was other activity. As the balloon lifted off a cannon saluted from Mousehold where, many years later, an aerodrome was established. Watchers in Norwich had the balloon in view for something like one and a half hours, and an observer, four miles from the city, saw through his telescope 'one person climb up among the netting, as if to adjust something'. The balloon took a northerly course, reaching an altitude of 8,000 ft.

Over Gunton Park, we are told, Mr. Green, who was not quite sure of his position, was able to call to people for bearings. All the time the seven-man crew had their eyes on the North Sea. Preparations were therefore made to descend at Metton, and the landing was accomplished, whereupon the aeronauts were invited to dine and sleep at Felbrigg Hall, near Cromer, but declined as they had friends waiting at Norwich. With farewells all round the party set off for the city in a carriage and four, the Norfolk Hotel being reached at 10.30 p.m. Then they 'partook of a splendid champagne supper'.

On October 15, 1785, a balloon ascent was made from Angel Hill, Bury St. Edmunds, by a Captain Poole. The ascent was described as 'remarkably even and gradual' in an easterly direction. After an hour the balloon became a mere dot in the sky 20 miles from the town and three miles high.

In The Athenaeum, Bury St. Edmunds, today is a pictorial record of Captain Poole's flight. It is a water colour drawing by J. Kendall, a well known local artist and engraver, who was approaching his middle forties at the time. The drawing was one of the gifts from the collection of the late Prince Frederick Duleep Singh who lived at Elveden Hall. In the foreground of the painting, figures of those present were superimposed by the Suffolk artist and caricaturist, Henry W. Bunbury.

Cambridge has some stories to tell of early aviation, Midsummer Common having seen both balloons and aeroplanes. However, the earliest story I can trace concerns one Edward D. Clarke who came as an undergraduate, aged 16, to Jesus College in 1786. In his third year—that was 1789—Clarke constructed a balloon and when completed it was 'suspended for some days in the College Hall, of which it occupied the whole height'. Ballons by then, however, were not so unusual but Clarke, who was later to become the first Cambridge Professor of Minerology in 1808 and also University

---

*Charles Green made hundreds of ascents. His son George, who died in 1864, sometimes called Charles Green, jnr., made ascents. And so did other members of the Green family, William, Henry and James. There is no doubt that the Henry Green who ascended at Ipswich in 1827 belonged to that family of aeronauts.

Photograph taken at the time of the first balloon ascent made near the old M.G.N. railway station at Beaconfield Recreation Ground, Great Yarmouth. *C. R. Temple*

Librarian in 1817, somehow managed to create intense interest throughout Cambridge 'respecting the fate of his experiment'.

On the appointed day Clarke had the balloon brought to the grass plot within the cloisters where, we are told, it was 'happily launched by himself, amidst the applause of all ranks and degree of gownsmen, who had crowded the roof as well as the area of the cloisters, and filled the contiguous apartments of the Master's lodge'. Clarke, as he lifted off, waved his cap. Aboard the basket with him was a little freight—a kitten.

The balloon soared over the towers of the great gate, while men on horseback, who were to recover the balloon, cantered after it.

Ipswich, it appears, was behind Norwich in taking an interest in ballooning. *The Ipswich Journal* for October 6, 1827, published a small advertisement to the effect that a Mr. Henry Green had arranged to make an ascent in his 'Magnificent Balloon' at 3 p.m. on October 12, take off being from a meadow owned by Mr. B. Raymond, opposite Mr. Bayley's shipyard, in the parish of St. Clement's. Mr. Green rose at the appointed time and drifted to the coast. However, the grapnel would not hold in the sandy soil and the poor aeronaut, with one eye on the North Sea, was dragged along the ground for two miles. The balloon was finally arrested at Hollesley and a shaken Mr. Green was finally back on earth.

A well known Suffolk artist and engraver, J. Kendall, recorded the balloon ascent made on October 15, 1785 by Captain Poole from Bury St Edmunds. Figures of those present were superimposed by another Suffolk artist, the caricaturist Henry W. Bunbury.   *O. G. Jarman and Borough of Bury St Edmunds*

When, on May 21, 1956, seven man-lifting kites under the direction of Mr. S. F. L. Cody, grandson of 'Colonel' Samuel F. Cody, the air pioneer, were launched for a brief period at Hardwick Park, near Bury St. Edmunds, the event recalled the latter's lucky escape during a similar stunt at Bury St. Edmunds in December, 1902.

'Colonel' Cody, who in his early days travelled the country putting on stage plays of his own in any sort of building or barn, was keen on kite flying. At Bury St. Edmunds in 1902 he tested a new design before a crowd of over 500 in rough, changeable wind conditions. He made the mistake, which in later experiments he avoided, of beginning his ascent before the lifters were high enough to be clear of ground gusts and squalls. It was while he was at 200 ft. that the tier of kites riding above him suddenly made a giant sweep sideways, as a child's kite sometimes does, until they reached almost tree top level. Cody, in the process, was swung helplessly in an arc towards the ground, and seconds later was flung into the branches of an oak. He climbed down suffering from bruises and scratches and, no doubt, shock.

Not many years later—on August 7, 1913—'Colonel' Cody was flying round Laffan's Plain, Farnborough, when his aircraft broke up. He and his passenger were killed.

Aerial view of Norwich taken in 1918 from an aircraft on a visit to Norfolk from Martlesham Heath.
Mrs Anne Hammond

CHAPTER II

Early Aeroplane Experimenters

A VERY important aviation development close to East Anglia took place near Colchester in 1909. The man involved was J. E. Humphreys, of Wivenhoe, who had carried out experiments at the turn of the century involving a detailed study of the structure and mechanism which enable birds to fly. He then undertook man-carrying glider tests in Cornwall.

Finally, using the craftsmanship of Wivenhoe shipwrights and fitters, Humphreys made his first powered aircraft, it being kept in a hangar on the marshes. But his amphibious biplane, believed to be the first project of its kind in the world, was, however, a failure. Within three months of this disappointment he built a monoplane —I have a trailing edge portion of a wing rib from the machine—and made preparations to enter the *Daily Mail* competition for a prize of £1,000 for the first Briton to fly a mile in a closed circuit in an all-British aeroplane. However, in trying to get off the ground in October, 1909, from totally unsuitable marshland, his dream aircraft crashed. Apparently an advanced type of construction was used and it was said that the monoplane was 'well in advance of its British contemporaries in 1909'. A year or two later, financially crippled, Humphreys, the pioneer, faded from the record.

In 1911 the Aeroplane Company, under Captain J. D. B. Fulton, R.A., flew to Hardwick, near Cambridge, and Thetford. This was early in the Aeroplane Company's history, for one of the pilots, Captain C. J. Burke, Royal Irish Regiment, who had learnt to fly Farmans in France and was attached to the Balloon School at Farnborough in advance of the formation of the Air Battalion, only started flying the aeroplane in January, 1911. Captain Fulton, who did the cross country flight to East Anglia, had his own Bleriot monoplane and was selected for attachment to the Company. On April 1, 1911, the Balloon School was reorganised as the Air Battalion. It had the specific duty of training officers and men in the handling of all forms of aircraft and provided a small body of expert airmen from which air units for war could be formed. This early military flying training laid a foundation for the future air service.

With the start of British aviation in 1910 the novelty of flying, if only in a series of leaps and bounds, caught the imagination of many. At Beccles, for instance, there were two separate ventures. Mr. Eugene C. Ulph, who is the honorary Borough Archivist, in telling me in 1969 that these early flights were attempted from Beccles Common, said: 'I was mad keen on these early aeroplanes and probably saw all that went on, living as I did at the time with my grandparents at the cottage on Boney's Island on the Common. My only regret is that none or few of the technical details ever came to my knowledge such as make of engines and horse power, but then details of design would not be easily apparent to a lad of 10.

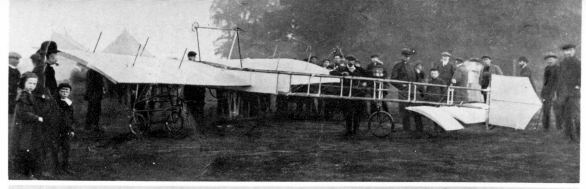

The King Monoplane on Beccles Common. In the upper photograph the tentage on the left may well have been used as a hangar whilst the trees on the right form what is known as Boney's Island.

Borough of Beccles

'However, one morning at breakfast grandfather announced, "the aeroplane is coming today", the large marquee had already been erected by the west side of the plantation, and quite how I endured sitting in school that morning I'll never know. Anyhow, on the stroke of 12, I was out and almost ran home, and there by the stables stood "The Thing". I can see it now: its bamboo frame, tapering off towards the tail, its wings and rudder removed as it had been brought over from Benacre on a horse drawn lorry. I suppose it was a kind of Bleriot monoplane, square tipped wings though. I almost kissed the fuselage, for here at last was an aeroplane, as you must remember at that time we had possibly seen but two or three in flight.

'Our Beccles aeroplane was owned by a man named King* and despite its many trial runs never left the ground. During a severe gale one Saturday evening both marquee and plane were wrecked, the wreckage being carted away on the Monday morning. That ended Mr. King's attempt at flying from Beccles Common.'

At this stage in our story it is worth recalling that in 1910-1911, which was the period of the first Beccles experiments, Major Lindsay Lloyd had made the inside of the famous motor track at Brooklands, Surrey, into a first class aerodrome. It was the starting and finishing point of the 1911 Circuit of Britain for a £10,000 prize put up by Lord Northcliffe. The year 1911 was also the year in which the fighting services began flying. In fact, the Admiralty generously allowed three naval officers, Lieutenants

*Mr. H. S. Sawyer, of Wrentham, Suffolk, told me in 1970: 'An aeroplane was made at Lowestoft and as far as I am aware the engine for it was built by a Mr. Talbot who eventually ran Zephyr Pistons. He was apparently with a Mr. Alec King who later formed A.K. Diesels Ltd. A machine was assembled on the Benacre-Kessingland denes but did not fly: it crashed into a hedge'.

This airscrew, held by Mr Christopher Morris, is believed to have been associated with the flying experiments at Beccles before the First World War. The close-up picture on the right shows the roughly hewn appearance of that airscrew.

C. F. Morris

Charles R. Samson, R. Gregory and Arthur M. Longmore, and a Royal Marine, Captain E. L. Gerrard, to draw full pay while they were taught to fly at the Royal Aero Club on the Isle of Sheppey, Kent, on Short biplanes.

It was on June 29, 1911, that Mr. Ulph saw the second flying venture on Beccles Common. He told me: 'A Merchant Navy officer—a Captain H. A. Sanders* of Lowestoft—had built a biplane and after a run or two at Benacre brought his plane to a hangar he had built on a marsh on the west side of the common. The captain was a frequent visitor to our cottage, also the nearby golf club, so I saw and heard much of the second venture. The machine's chief defect at the start were two chain driven

*The *East Anglian Daily Times* for February 8, 1960, under 'Fifty Years Ago', recalled that in 1910 'a Mr. Sanders' was testing at Kessingland an aeroplane which was entirely British made, it being pointed out that other contemporary aircraft were 'largely composed of foreign components'. It had a '300 h.p. motor . . . specially made by Messrs. Brooke, of Lowestoft'. But the test ended in near disaster for the pilot. For at a speed of 35 m.p.h. and at a height of 20 ft. the aeroplane collided with a line of telephone wires—the skids caught the wires—and the machine was completely wrecked, 'hardly any portion of the intricate wooden framework remaining intact'. The pilot escaped serious injury. Date of the crash was February 13, 1910.

propellers, the engine being positioned on the lower wing behind the pilot's seat. Of course this resulted in a series of chain breaks getting nowhere. Then Captain Sanders dropped the idea of twin propellers, raised the engine, and the propeller was driven direct from the engine. This was a vast improvement.

'I'd say that the machine was a pusher type. Anyhow, the biplane began to leave the ground, a few feet at first, gradually increasing on further trials until one evening it took off, rising some 50 to 100 feet, scaled the butts, turned, crossed the Worlingham marshes and reached the railway line as a train was approaching from Lowestoft. The plane continued overhead and for several moments plane and train were neck-and-neck though, of course, the plane's speed told in the end. I can well remember the following day's *Eastern Daily Press* news bill outside the news-agents: "Beccles Aeroplane races Train".

'Alas! the train reached its destination safely—the aeroplane didn't. After reaching the Black Dam rail crossing it lost height and struck a tree, damaging one of its wings. However, the machine was repaired and further trials followed. I should say practically all the plane's trials were carried out by a Lieutenant Parke, R.N., loaned from Aldershot, as evidently the services were keen to assist any pioneering of flight. Short Bros. supplied two experienced mechanics, Bert Wanham and Tom Jobling.'

After the crash at Kessingland (see footnote p. 25) the Sanders Type 1 biplane was rebuilt at Beccles to become, as shown above, a Saunders Type 2. Lieutenant Wilfred Parke made flights in it from Beccles Common. He crashed to his death over Middlesex in 1912. *C. F. Morris*

The year 1912, quite apart from the fact that Beccles people saw what must have been their first aeroplane crash, is historic because it also saw the formation of the Royal Flying Corps, which consisted of a Naval and Military Wing, to supply air arms for both Services. Various commercial firms were formed to make aeroplanes, the Navy believing in developing private enterprises by competition, to sharpen the brains of the designers.

Thus Mr. Ulph's inference that the Services were keen to assist experimenters is correct. Lieutenant Wilfred Parke, for that was the officer who came to Beccles, lost his life the same year at Wembley Park, Middlesex, when a Handley Page monoplane on a flight from Hendon to Oxford crashed on December 15, 1912. With him died Frederick Handley Page's chief assistant, Mr. Arkell A. Hardwick, and the crash was a tragedy for aviation in general and for the company in particular. Lieutenant Parke was at the time 'a very important figure in the aviation world'.

Flying gondola built by the author's father at Beccles in 1938. If the Second World War had not intervened it would probably have been developed as a harnessed trainer.   *M. E. Elliott*

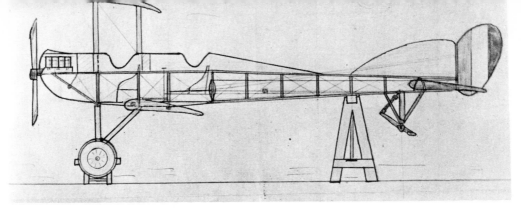

Side elevation of a B.E.2e drawn by a Beccles pupil pilot in the First World War.   *Author*

Lieutenant Parke, who was the son of a Dorsetshire parson, between the spring of 1911 and the end of 1912, flew no less than 29 different kinds of aeroplanes—a record for those early days. When he was killed at the age of 23 he left an unpublished book called *Aviaticanda* which described the tests he had carried out.

Apparently the Sanders biplane, which Lieutenant Parke tested at Beccles, first of all had an American Alvaston engine, then an eight cylinder E.N.V. engine lent by the celebrated 'Colonel' Samuel F. Cody, Anglo-American aviation pioneer.

Airscrews, the term propeller came later, were a problem. Earlier airscrews used at Beccles were hand hewn from solid blocks of Russian pine by Captain Sanders' own carpenters, Tom Palmer, of Gorleston, and Willie Burgess, of Beccles. Later mahogany airscrews from Paris were used. On account of the accuracy and finish which was necessary the manufacture of wooden airscrews represented the culmination of the woodworkers' art.

In 1966 Mr. James Hoseason, of the Waveney Flying Group, based at the old U.S.A.A.F. airfield at Seething, Norfolk, told me: 'It is true that we have some very early propellers* in our possession at Seething airfield, one of which was handmade locally for an original aircraft built privately at Beccles. . .'.

But Captain Sanders had a further attempt at flight before leaving Beccles for good. Another machine—the Sanders Biplane No. 2—was built by the Sanders Aeroplane Company, and taken by road to Benacre flower show, but was wrecked while attempting to take off. The pilot had a lucky escape. With money running out the Sanders Aeroplane Company, which might have changed the face of Beccles, was wound up on the eve of World War I in 1914. The Company's demise was regretted as it was generally considered that Captain Sanders was making progress.

Mr. Ulph said that 'a Mr. Basil Elliott who was a keen enthusiast' was photographed alongside the King monoplane of 1911. This was one of my father's brothers,

*Mr. Christopher Morris, of Hatfield, Herts. told me in 1970: 'The propeller I have is one of a batch of three sold in an auction in Beccles some 10 years ago, origin unknown . . . I recovered it five years ago, and re-varnished it. I also had to re-glue the laminations. The other two, unfortunately, have been lost without trace in that short space of time'.

Basil W. Elliott, who is buried in St. Michael's Cemetery, Astoria, Long Island, New York, the stone bearing the inscription 'British Soldier'. When I mentioned the fact to another uncle of mine in 1970 he said that Basil Elliott was most certainly interested in the King monoplane and wanted very much to become mechanic to King. However, my grandfather, Alexander Elliott, who had been brought up as a steam engineer, could see no future in the King experiments and refused to have his son indentured. Basil Elliott thereupon left for America, later crossing to Canada, where he eventually joined the 24th Canadians, V.R.C., being present in the storming of Vimy Ridge in 1917.

Many years later—in 1937-1938—my father started to design a powered flying gondola for us in our garden in Fair Close, Beccles, a short distance from the common. The gondola was suspended from a boom attached to a central post about which it revolved. A 1 h.p. engine, driving a small home-made sycamore propeller, which I have still, propelled the roundabout at 30 or so m.p.h. The oil was mixed with the petrol, and on a hot day we felt as ill as Harry Hawker must have been when overcome by sun and fumes at Great Yarmouth.

Gaumont British News, on hearing of the Beccles 'flying machine', made a film which was shown quite widely. Newspapers and magazines in this country and abroad published photographs of the novelty, and one picture, I remember, concluded a pictorial history of flight, starting in 1500, which appeared in the *News Chronicle* on January 5, 1939.

What became of the roundabout? Well, my father had plans for fitting a balanced boom to the contraption so that, by means of weights and proper controls, the gondola could be made to have the movements of an aeroplane. But the war came, and in the 1950s the roundabout was scrapped, the propeller being the only surviving relic.

In the middle of May, 1912, the *Daily Mail* announced the 'Daily Mail Flying Tour' —a 13 week series of air journeys from place to place for the purpose of demonstrating the progress made in the construction of aeroplanes.

M. Henri Salmet, the well known aviator, who on March 7 of that year had made the first return flight London (Hendon) to Paris and back in one day, accepted an invitation to become the first of the *Daily Mail* flying men, and within a few days had started on a tour of the west country in a Bleriot monoplane. Later in 1912—on Saturday, August 10—he visited Ipswich, and the *Daily Mail* on August 12 had this to say: 'Thousands of people ... waited for M. Salmet, the *Daily Mail* airman, at Ipswich, whither he flew from Felixstowe. They were rewarded by witnessing a fine circuit of the town by the airman at a height of 1,000 ft. M. Salmet eventually landed on Gippeswyck Park Farm, where he was welcomed by the owner, Mr. J. A. Smith, prominent Suffolk agriculturist. The 12 mile journey from Felixstowe had occupied 10 minutes'. Gippeswyck Farm is situated on the south west side of Ipswich near Belstead Road.

Henri Salmet, the first of the *Daily Mail* flying men, at Ipswich on Saturday, August 10, 1912. Watched by thousands of people he made a circuit of the town, before landing at Gippeswyck Park Farm on the south west side of Ipswich.   *Leonard Sewell*

The landing spot was marked with a large white linen cross. Before alighting, M. Salmet gave a series of exhibition flights over the ground, where 2,000 waited, 'darting over the heads of the people with marvellous skill and intrepidity'. Once down the crowd pressed round his machine, and M. Salmet, on seeing a lad tampering with the back portion of his aeroplane, pointed to the biceps of his arm, and jokingly remarked: 'If I jump down, my boy, there is two hundred pounds here'. The aviator had the support of his mechanic, Mr. Bertram May, who told the crowd that the Bleriot cost complete £900 of which the 50 h.p. seven cylinder Gnome engine cost over half—£500. The airscrew—it was of Spanish mahogany—cost £20. Apart from the cost of the machine, what did it look like? The Bleriot had a span of 25 ft., was covered with rubberised and waterproofed fabric, and its airframe was constructed of steel tube, ash and bamboo.

It is said that the first man to fly over Norwich in an aeroplane was Bentfield C. Hucks, great pre-1914 pilot, who was also one of the *Daily Mail* flying men. We find that on August 10, 1912, Hucks flew a Bleriot—it bore the tail number 16 and was named 'Firefly'—from Gorleston to Church Lane, Eaton. The *Eastern Daily Press*

B. C. Hucks' Bleriot, *Firefly* in Norfolk.   *George Swain*

B. C. Hucks the first British pilot to loop-the-loop. *George Swain*

for August 12, 1912, noted: 'The first sighting of the monoplane sent a thrill of excitement through the crowd. It appeared but a dark speck moving almost imperceptibly through the vast spaces of the horizon. . .'. Once over the landing ground there were wild cheers of 'Bravo, Hucks'. Hucks was feted when he landed, many women wanting him to sign autographs, but he politely declined.

On his flight from Great Yarmouth to Acle, Hucks followed the main road and afterwards the railway line. Due to a thick brown mist he only picked up Norwich because the river with the sun shining on it 'looked like molten gold'. He was in the air for 20 minutes.

Not long after his Eaton demonstration, on May 14, 1914, Hucks visited Hethersett race course in his Bleriot. His purpose this time, he was the first British pilot to loop-the-loop, was to show local people just that. He had looped over 400 times before his visit to Hethersett. The *Eastern Daily Press* reported next day that he 'accomplished several times over his marvellous feats of upside down flying and looping the loop'. Hucks was accompanied by an up and coming young pupil pilot, Mr. Marcus D. Manton, aged 20, of Sheffield, who had learnt to fly two years before. 'Further looping', the report said, 'intensified the crowd's astonishment, and when Hucks again recovered a normal position and sailed off for a brief trip across country people roused themselves as if from a dream'. The stunting was watched by the crew of a naval machine which had come over from Great Yarmouth.

Incidentally, Captain Hucks, as he became later, invented the Hucks starter for aircraft. It consisted of a revolving screw mounted on a Ford chassis and operated by a chain drive. The screw was attached to the propeller hub and rotated the engine into life. Hitherto aircraft engines had to be started by hand swinging of the propeller.

In order to perfect the looping art Hucks first of all experimented by hanging upside down in the cockpit of his aircraft for 15 minutes. Then followed other loop-the-loop successes so that Claude Grahame-White, in honour of the 'looping mania', gave an upside-down dinner at the Royal Automobile Club on March 20, 1914. Hucks was one of the guests of honour, and by all accounts it was an odd dinner, for the tables were upside down, their legs pointing upwards. Hucks sat under a large mirror which reflected him upside down!

In September, 1912 army manoeuvres took place in East Anglia at Snarehill, Thetford, which has an important place in the history of the growth of air power and the R.A.F. Trenchard's* eyes were opened wide to the military possibilities of flying after his experience as an air observer during the manoeuvres.

It is recorded that Longmore† and five other pilots were chosen to spot for the northern force under General Sir James Grierson. Longmore carrying Trenchard in a Maurice Farman Longhorn flew from Thetford on the first day of the exercise. His orders?: to locate General Sir Douglas Haig's advancing southern force. Trenchard spotted 'weapons and equipment glittering at every step'. He reported back to General Grierson within an hour but there was no fast way of recalling the cavalry of the northern force so that they could be deployed in the right area. Longmore and Trenchard were therefore detailed to carry the message to them.

The pair in their Farman eventually sighted horse-drawn transport and the 'flashing points of cavalry lances' by the hedges of the Newmarket road. The Farman circled, having found both friend and foe from the air, and the airmen knew that 'a regiment of cavalry was no substitute for a single reconnaissance aircraft'. Trenchard gave the message to General Briggs of the Northern force who acted on it at once.

Afterwards it was admitted officially that the manoeuvres had been largely influenced by the 'intervention of aircraft' which secured the initiative for General Grierson. At the same time the pilots on General Haig's side— the southern force— were no less active.

Sir Walter Raleigh, the air historian, commented: 'In the course of a few days the aeroplanes rose into such esteem that they were asked to verify information which had been brought in by the cavalry'.

*Lord Trenchard, G.C.B., O.M., G.C.V.O., D.S.O., who was born in 1873 and died in 1956, was affectionately known as 'Father of the Royal Air Force'. He was the first officer to be created a Marshal of the R.A.F. Lord Trenchard was Chief of Air Staff from 1918 to 1929 and was responsible for the permanent organisation of the R.A.F. 1919, and the foundation of the R.A.F. Apprentice Training Scheme at Halton in 1920.

†Air Marshal Sir Arthur M. Longmore, G.C.B., D.S.O., was one of a small number of specially selected pilots who were trained in 1911. Born in 1885, he entered the Royal Navy in 1900, held several important commands, and retired from the R.A.F. in 1942 and died in 1970.

When exactly did these great manoeuvres, in which hundreds of British troops were involved, take place? Apparently the build up of men and equipment started some time before September 15, 1912. The first day of the 'battle' was Monday, September 16, and the local press noted that Monday was an ideal day for flying—'a calm, still, hazy day of early autumn'. Little did the reporter know how true his words were to become in history when he added: 'There seemed a hush over Nature like that which precedes a storm'. Interestingly the press noted that two aeroplanes from 'Blue' Force—General Grierson's force—were captured near Water Hall on the Newmarket-Barton Mills road by 'Red' Force troops. The 'battle' went on for three days—until Wednesday, September 18.

We have already referred to 'Colonel' Cody's visit to Bury St. Edmunds in 1902 —the year the Boer War ended. Well, he appeared at the 1912 manoeuvres full of the joys of life, for his biplane, which landed at Hardwick, near Cambridge, on September 15, had just won the War Office competition, both international and British sections, and £5,000 prize money. He was, as usual, keen to talk to the press, and he told them that he had visited the Cambridge area during the Boer War while he was touring as the villain in 'The Klondyke Nugget'. They performed in a wooden building on the outskirts of Cambridge. That was when he was experimenting with man-lifting kites in the hope of developing a flying machine—a dream, in fact, which he achieved not many years later.

One of the two B.E. biplanes, which acted as scouts in the Thetford area manoeuvres of 1912, after landing at Worlington.   *Donald Parker*

Air Marshal Sir Arthur Longmore told me just before he died in 1970, that Trenchard acted as his observer and that they flew to Thetford by way of Oxford and Hardwick, near Cambridge. About half a dozen aeroplanes were with the northern force.

Sir Arthur, in his book *From Sea to Sky,* recalled that they flew from any convenient field—grass or stubble—in the area. On one day they flew six hours on tactical reconnaissance. Of one incident, he said: 'Getting out of that field, however, I chipped the airscrew on one of those stick erections which gamekeepers use to stop poachers dragging their nets across the field. Luckily my ground organisation was equal to the occasion, for I had a spare airscrew strapped to my private car'. On his last landing during the 1912 manoeuvres, Sir Arthur broke a longeron which affected the tail structure of his Farman. 'We found the nearest blacksmith', he wrote, 'blew up his fire, and during the night . . . made a metal sleeve with which we fixed that longeron'. Then the manoeuvres ended near Little Thurlow not far from Clare.

Barton Mills, near Mildenhall, where his father owned a flour mill, was the birth place of the late John Lankester Parker*, one of the early British aviators, who was a test pilot for nearly 30 years and handled such famous four engined aircraft as the Short Sunderland, well-known at Felixstowe, and the Short Stirling bomber, the miniature of which was test flown from Martlesham Heath in the late 1930s.

How did he come to take up flying? Mr. Lankester Parker related in the early 1960s: 'It was in 1910 that the urge first came to me. Out for a Sunday afternoon walk with my elder brother,we were taking a rest on a railway bank when our attention was taken by a magnificent exhibition of flying by some rooks . . . After a while, my brother has since reminded me, I exclaimed with unusual vehemence: "I am going to fly". Somehow he knew it was not the passing whim of a 14 year old.

*The family have a farming ancestry but have been millers at Barton Mills since the 1880s.

Air Marshal Sir Arthur M. Longmore, seen here in the cockpit of an early aeroplane, held certificate No. 72 of the Royal Aero Club dated April 1911. This was the oldest held by any serving officer of the R.A.F. during the Second World War.
Lord Trenchard

During the 1912 manoeuvres Trenchard (with pipe) and Longmore (in deer-stalker) flew together and are shown here during a lull in the "fighting".   *Lord Trenchard*

'Two years elapsed before I saw an aeroplane for the first time. It was during the military manoeuvres in the autumn of 1912 that two B.E. biplanes*, acting as scouts, landed in fields at Worlington near my home in Suffolk . . . Soon I joined Vickers Flying School and qualified in June, 1914'.

Mr. Donald Parker, the aviator's brother, writing from Mildenhall in 1970, told me: 'J.L. and his brothers as schoolboys, some 60 years ago, were desperately keen on flying and would cycle to the neighbourhood of Hendon on the off chance of seeing an aeroplane in the sky.

'After a period as instructor on seaplanes at Windermere, and later as a freelance test pilot with Clifford Prodger, in 1914, J.L. went to Short Bros. as a test pilot. But, having arrived at Eastchurch, Horace Short said he was not going to have "bits of boys flying his aeroplanes". But my brother kept worrying him, and eventually Horace Short said: "Well, take up that bomber, and break your b....y neck". J. L. promptly put three bombers through their tests, and remained as Short's chief test pilot for some 30 years'.

In 1918 Parker flew a Short Shirl, a new torpedo biplane, to Martlesham Heath —it was his first sight of the establishment—but due to a faulty throttle, which caused the engine to run full blast, he flew to Suffolk in a steady climb to avoid over-speeding. Thus he arrived over Martlesham Heath, not at a reasonable two or three thousand feet, but at 12,000 ft. The only way to get down, then, was to switch off the engine and glide. This he did and landed well and truly in the centre of the famous testing ground.

*Mr. Lankester Parker believed they were flown by 'Captain C. A. H. Longcroft and Captain de Havilland (later Sir Geoffrey)'.

Sheet music of Ezra Read's Waltzes *Aeroplane*
dedicated to Colonel Cody.　　　　　*Author*

On May 19, 1913, Mr. Norman C. Spratt flew from Southwold Common in a Deperdussin monoplane. It seems that he spent 12 days at Southwold, the last few of which were enforced owing to the strong wind. His ambition was to fly from Southwold to Hendon, so at 5 o'clock on the morning of Monday, May 19, he took off with his mechanic, Mr. Barrs. But the flight unfortunately was ruined by engine failure.

The *East Anglian Daily Times* for May 20, 1913, said: 'It was the intention of Mr. Spratt to make a non-stop flight to Hendon, but his engine failed at 5.40 a.m. and he had to come to ground on Eyke Common. He had drifted four miles out of his course, and had only made 20 miles in 40 minutes . . . There was a strong cross wind blowing, and when his engine failed, Mr. Spratt was at an altitude of about 2,300 ft.'.

What did Mr. Spratt do in the end? Well, he left his Deperdussin at Woodbridge, having had it brought in from Eyke, and Mr. C. D. Castell, of Wickham Market, arranged transport for the monoplane to Hendon. The machine had a wing span of 28 ft., and the airframe was of ash and spruce. The 60 h.p. engine, which gave it a speed of 65 m.p.h., was covered with an aluminium cowling, the cockpit floor and ventral fairing was of plywood, and its fuselage, wings and tail of oiled cotton. Three Deperdussins, incidentally, were among the aeroplanes entered for the British Military Trials in August, 1912.

The early attempts at flying at Beccles caused several young men to think of joining the air arm. One youngster, who was born near Beccles in 1898, preserved his R.F.C./R.A.F. workshop notebooks which were compiled during his training as a pupil pilot.

When a special exhibition to commemorate the Royal Flying Corps was held in 1962 at the Imperial War Museum, London, some of the Beccles documents, including an original drawing of a B.E. 2 cockpit layout and a side elevation of the same machine, were exhibited alongside an original document relating to Claude Grahame-White's appointment as a flight commander 'in His Majesty's Navy' on September 13, 1914. Grahame-White, who was a British pioneer pilot, first became interested in flying in 1909 when the Beccles pupil pilot was 11.

The B.E.2 drawings are of special interest because the type, which was designed by Mr. Geoffrey de Havilland, was the first aeroplane to be officially adopted by the

John Lankester Parker (right) in the cockpit of a Short flying boat with Mr. Winston Churchill in 1928.
Donald Parker

Army Airship "Beta", seen in flight, took part in the 1912 manoeuvres at Thetford.   *Peter Spencer*

R.F.C. and was also the first to land in France in August, 1914. At the start of its career it had no ailerons and was controlled laterally by wing warping. It was never designed to carry any gun mountings so the first B.E. 2s had to be defended by means of a hand held rifle from the rear cockpit! The B.E.2, incidentally, was the aeroplane which was most successful against Zeppelins. Although considerable controversy surrounded this machine not only for home defence but for use in the field, in the long run it more than justified itself. It started out with a 90 h.p. Raf engine.

In the first decade or so of the 20th century, it has been pointed out, aircraft started to appear at demonstrations in East Anglia. The year 1910, in fact, saw the beginning of British aviation. In the previous year a few foreign aviators had come over here and shown us how to fly, and a few early pioneers, such as Mr. A. V. Roe, the Short brothers, Mr. Geoffrey de Havilland, Mr. Robert Blackburn, and Mr. Howard Wright, had made experimental flying machines. However, they could hardly be said to have flown.

One wonders how much these early experimenters influenced the siting of airfields* in later years. When the Great War started in 1914 a survey was made of suitable places along the East Coast for seaplanes and landplanes. Among the spots selected were Great Yarmouth, Hickling Broad and Felixstowe for seaplanes, Snarehill, Aldeburgh, Sedgeford, Holt, Cromer, Narborough, Bacton, Covehithe and Burgh Castle for landplanes.

Miss Dorothy Keable, who was born at Earsham, recalled in 1969; 'The airstrip at Earsham was a 24 acre field belonging to Earsham Park . . . between Earsham-Homersfield main road . . . Men in khaki uniform lived in huts on the field. It was an emergency landing field. We raced to see a plane come down one Sunday afternoon— a very frail little thing of wood, canvas and string. It was the first we'd ever seen at close quarters. That would have been about 1915 or 1916'. Here it is interesting to

*It is interesting to note that in 1909 Noel Pemberton Billing, one of the early pioneers, laid out an aerodrome at Fambridge roughly halfway between Maldon and Rochford, Essex.

note that no permanent airfield resulted from the temporary visitation at Earsham. What, I wonder, decided the issue in the first place? Did an officer decide that it would be nice to live on top of one's job? Did a convenient inn—or an attractive village maiden—affect the judgement of the survey party?

On the other hand, I recall that in the early 1930s a recognised landing area existed near Ringsfield Road, Beccles, and joy flights were staged there. A few years later, in 1937, a Hawker Hind light bomber force-landed on the very site. It seems likely, therefore, that for the first 20 or so years navigation maps included all known suitable landing spots and that this information, so vital to the pilot in trouble, was culled from experience and handed on.

Some years ago I was shown a most interesting little manual—the 1914 Training Manual of the Royal Flying Corps, price 3d., which was issued 'by command of the Lords Commissioners of the Admiralty and by command of the Army Council for the guidance of all concerned'.

The manual devoted a paragraph to landing places: 'Aeroplanes can land on or rise from short grass, stubble, or dry plough, but the first is best . . . When the ground is level with a hard surface and the hedges do not exceed 5 feet in height, a field of 200 yards square (about 9 acres) is sufficient for any but a very fast aeroplane to land in . . . If an aeroplane has to land over trees or telegraph wires a horizontal distance equal to 12 times the height of the obstacle should be added to the 200 yards. These measurements are based on the supposition that the aeroplane will rise and land against any wind that may be blowing . . . If there is a wire fence or iron railing round the landing place, pieces of cloth or blankets should be hung on it to make it visible from the air'.

Later, as already recorded, joy flights were given in the early 1930s from a field near Ringsfield Road, Beccles. Among our family snaps are two or three showing my late R.A.F. brother, then eight or nine, in the rear cockpit of a visiting Avro 504K biplane, complete with skid to keep the propeller tips clear of the ground when landing.

Norman Spratt's Deperdussin which he flew from Southwold Common on May 91, 1913.   *F. Jenkins*

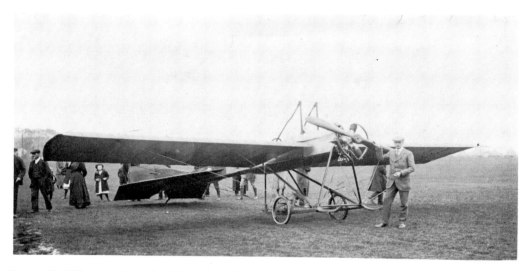

Mr. A. G. Miller with Spratt's 60 h.p. Deperdussin Monoplane at Southwold, May 1913. *F. Jenkins*

Mr. A. J. Jackson, aviation historian and expert on Avro aircraft since 1908, when shown a photograph of G-ABAU, commented: 'I was delighted to receive the photograph of the Avro 504 G-ABAU as it has always eluded me—and in this respect is unique among Avros. This machine had a relatively short civil life of about 18 months. It was owned and probably flown by a Mr. H. Sinclair, who lived at Clapham Common, and who probably converted it for joy-riding at Croydon. Your allusion to its East Anglian joy-riding activities is correct—the certificate of airworthiness was issued in August, 1930. I saw it in a field at Chelmsford on May 17, 1932, and it crashed soon afterwards, but where I have not yet discovered'.

The military version of the Avro 504—hundreds of the type were sold at the end of the Great War for civilian use—made history on November 21, 1914, when three used by the Royal Navy attacked the Zeppelin works and sheds at Friedrichshafen on Lake Constance. Their claim to fame came about because they were the first aircraft to carry a mechanically operated bomb release mechanism. Although the mechanism was 'A Heath Robinson job', this was A. V. Roe's description, the three Avros, after a long and cold flight, made an effective bombing attack, only one bomb failing to release.

CHAPTER III

Seaplanes at Great Yarmouth

IN THE autumn of 1912 the authorities looked at the Norfolk coast for a suitable air station for seaplanes. A site on the south denes at Great Yarmouth was chosen after other sites had been looked at on the north denes, between Caister and Great Yarmouth, and on the foreshore south of Gorleston. As was the case at Bacton, higher up the coast, the existence on the south denes at Great Yarmouth of Coastguard accommodation proved attractive.

The Corporation of Great Yarmouth agreed to rent out five acres between Marine Parade and the beach, some 1,000 yards south of the Nelson Column*. The total charge at the agricultural rate of £2 10s. per acre was £12 10s. However, the denes were not at all suitable for an aerodrome as the strip was very narrow—about a quarter of a mile wide and half a mile long. On the east side, if one misjudged the landing area, was the sea; on the south side the harbour; on the west side the River Yare, and, very dangerously, the Nelson Column on the north side. Mixed up with the landing area were the now vanished fish pickling plots.

A few months after the survey party had decided on Great Yarmouth the Admiralty announced, on April 13, 1913, a number of naval appointments for the air station. Lieutenant R. Gregory, who had held the post of Squadron Commander in the Naval Wing of the Royal Flying Corps at Felixstowe, was appointed to command the Great Yarmouth group of air stations which eventually extended north and south of the port, all being sited close to the coast. Two days later, on April 15, the station was commissioned, the official headquarters was opened at 25 Regent Street and the first hangar of steel and canvas was erected. The initial manpower was small—three officers and five naval ratings.

The first machine to arrive at Great Yarmouth was a Maurice Farman land plane No. 69. It was flown in by Lieutenant Christopher L. Courtney†, Flight Commander, Great Yarmouth, on May 31 of that year. Lieutenant Courtney, who was accompanied by a mechanic named Hackney, had set out from Hendon in the morning and had passed over Ipswich, Woodbridge and Saxmundham. At Carlton Colville, just outside Lowestoft, however, they had to descend for petrol. Shortly afterwards they reached the south denes, landing at 10 p.m., the flight having taken the best part of a day. A month after the Farman's arrival, No. 69 had to make a forced landing near Hopton in the hands of Lieutenant T. S. Cresswell, who on June 4, 1914, lost his life over the Solent when the wings of his seaplane folded up in flight.

C. F. Snowden Gamble in his book, *The Story of a North Sea Air Station,* said; 'The difficulties experienced during the daytime, both in taking off and landing

---

*The pillar is 144 ft. high. The first stone was laid on August 15, 1817. A move by the airmen to have the prongs of Britannia's trident marked by a light was rejected. *An Historical Guide to Great Yarmouth in Norfolk with the Most Remarkable Events Recorded of that Town,* published in 1817, noted in respect of the south denes: 'The soil so readily absorbs the heaviest showers, that immediately on their ceasing, every one may walk there without experiencing the slightest inconvenience'. No doubt the ideal turf conditions influenced the survey party in 1912 just as much as the presence of Coastguard accommodation.

†Born in 1890, he was in the R.N.A.S. from 1912 to 1918 and afterwards in the R.A.F., reaching the rank of Air Chief Marshal by 1945.

An 1918 aerial view of Great Yarmouth Air Station in which a number of land and sea planes are visible.

P. *Button*

machines, naturally were increased greatly at night time, for in the darkness the only guide that a pilot had for taking off his machine was the light of a torch held in the air by an air mechanic standing at the far end of the denes.'

In 1913 flying boats began to develop. Thomas O. M. Sopwith learnt to fly in 1910 working with S. Saunders, of Cowes, who had built many racing motor boats for him, and produced the first amphibian flying boat. At the same time Captain Ernest Bass and John C. Porte, then a lieutenant, who was to become well known at Felixstowe, brought over a Curtiss flying boat from the United States.

In July, 1913, Great Yarmouth air station took part in the great naval manoeuvres when, for the first time, aircraft were used by the Royal Navy with the fleet at sea. 'War' was declared on July 23, and two submarines were spotted from the air off Cromer.

Great Yarmouth had contact with Harry Hawker*, the celebrated Australian pioneer pilot, who was killed in a crash on July 12, 1921. That was in 1913 when he entered for the famous seaplane trial organized by the *Daily Mail*—a competition worth £5,000 in prize money. The distance to be flown was about 1,500 miles, and the course, which was divided into nine stages, was Southampton—Ramsgate—Great Yarmouth Scarborough — Aberdeen — Cromarty — Oban — Dublin — Falmouth — Southampton. The longest of these stretches was from Dublin to Falmouth, in Cornwall, a distance of 280 miles.

*H. G. (Harry) Hawker made the first attempt to fly across the North Atlantic Ocean in 1919. His companion was Commander K. Mackenzie Grieve, R.N., and 750 miles from the Irish coast their Sopwith biplane—it had a single engine—fell into the sea. For a week there was no news that a ship had picked them up.

Hawker, who left Southampton at 11.47 a.m., passed Felixstowe at 3.50 p.m., Lowestoft at 4.30 p.m., and touched down at Great Yarmouth seven minutes later. Excited crowds saw his Sopwith seaplane from Dovercourt, Aldeburgh and Southwold.

As things turned out the race was 'one of the most extraordinary experiences of Hawker's career'. On August 16, 1913, he took off from Southampton with one passenger, Mr. H. Kauper. He made good time until he reached Great Yarmouth. As Hawker stepped from the Sopwith seaplane he collapsed, 'having been overcome by the sun and fumes from the Green engine'. With head bandaged he rested at the naval air station.

That ended Hawker's first attempt to capture this valuable prize, but just over a week later, and only five days before the competition closed, he set off from Great Yarmouth and reached Seaham, County Durham, safely. From then on weather and other problems did their best to break the spirits of Hawker and Kauper. Ultimately Hawker flew over 1,000 miles in about 24 hours and, while he did not win the *Daily Mail* prize, he had performed so great a feat of flying that he was given a special prize of £1,000. The Royal Aero Club gave him its silver medal, and the club's bronze medal was awarded to his faithful passenger Kauper who continually fought illness during that testing flight.

As First Lord of the Admiralty, Mr. Winston Churchill, who took an exceptional interest in the aeroplane as a weapon, wrote to the Director of Works on November

Some aircraft from Great Yarmouth were fitted with Le Prieur rockets for use against Zeppelins. They were usually launched from rails attached to the interplane struts.   *Ministry of Defence*

An Avro K450 used for joy flights, picture probably 1926: remaining Great Yarmouth Air Station hanger in background.

C. R. Temple

7, 1913: 'You are to ascertain and report without delay what internal alterations are necessary to make the Coastguard stations at Calshot (Warsash), Grain Island, Felixstowe and Yarmouth suitable for accommodating the officers and men of the air stations. Only alterations that are absolutely necessary to be considered. Suitable accommodation for forming a small officers' mess is to be provided'.

The first war patrol was flown from Great Yarmouth on August 9, 1914. At its peak the station had 80 officers and 900 men. Pilots and groundcrews lived about one and a half miles from the actual sheds and airfield. When Zeppelins were reported the officers piled into cars and the ground-crews into lorries and raced along the front regardless of the hour. By mid-1918 so many aircraft, seaplanes and landplanes, were accommodated at Great Yarmouth that three hangars were put up at Burgh Castle and some Sopwith Camels and D.H.4s., under the command of Captain G.W.R. Fane, went there. Burgh Castle, incidentally, with her landing flares burning at night was sometimes mistaken by the Zeppelins for the main station at Great Yarmouth—which was the intention.

Great Yarmouth's fighters had a big front to cover. From Aldeburgh to Covehithe is 15 miles, Covehithe to Great Yarmouth 16 miles, Great Yarmouth to Bacton 20

First World War carrier pigeons played a big part in saving lives at Great Yarmouth and Felixstowe. This pigeon saved the lives of six airmen.
Dr. P. J. Hynes

miles, Bacton to Holt 18 miles, Holt to Hunstanton 25 miles, and Hunstanton to Narborough 18 miles. The seaplanes, which flew hundreds of miles, were away for many hours at a time.

In January, 1916, a considerable amount of night flying was done at Great Yarmouth with B.E.2cs. One aid to night flying tried was a string with a weight on. It was reeled out like an aerial and when it touched, as was hoped, the ground it lit a red lamp and started a buzzer ringing inside the cockpit! From experience it was found that the combination of these effects often led to the pilot making a heavier than ever landing and the well-meant aid was discarded.

Great Yarmouth air station got its first D.H. 4 in August, 1917, and the type performed a number of outstanding deeds while at the Norfolk station, the finest being the destruction at night of the new German Zeppelin L.70. The D.H. 4—Britain built 1,450 and America had orders for no less than 4,844 of this type in the Great War—was an orthodox biplane of wood construction but of high aerodynamic qualities.

On August 5/6, 1918, the last Zeppelin attack was made on this country. Once again East Anglia came into the picture. Five Zeppelins made for England that night, and at about 8 o'clock three were sighted from the Leman Tail lightship. The L.70, the leader, had on board Fregattenkapitan Peter Strasser, head of the German Airship Service, who had led the first airship raid on this country in 1915. At about 9.45 p.m. the L.70 was just north of Cromer, with the L.65 to her starboard and the L.53 to her port.

Thirteen machines rose from Great Yarmouth. Major Egbert Cadbury*, in a D.H. 4, with Captain R. Leckie as observer, went up at a little past 9 o'clock. At about

*Major (later Sir Egbert) Cadbury, D.S.C., D.F.C., who died in 1967, was a grandson of the founder of the chocolate firm which bears his name. He was born in 1893, and went to Trinity College, Cambridge.

17,000 feet the pair attacked the L.70 head on and slightly to port. Leckie fired into the airship's bows and a great hole was blown in the fabric. Fire soon enveloped the giant. People on the Norfolk coast saw the L.70 fall eight miles north of Wells and not far from the schooner *Amethyst*. Cadbury also damaged the L.65. Then the victorious D.H. 4 landed at Sedgeford in the north west corner of Norfolk where, in the darkness, Cadbury nearly collided with another aircraft. In addition, Cadbury was shaken to find that he had touched down with two 100 lb. bombs still in the racks. Of the L.70 very little survived. It was said that one of the crew was buried at Weybourne. What is certain is that the body of Leutnant zur See von Kruger, who belonged to the L.70 was picked up by the enemy off the Frisian coast. Pieces of the airship were washed ashore north of the Wash.

Meanwhile the L.56 and the L.63 approached Great Yarmouth at about 9 o'clock without being seen and flew north along the coast. Both airships apparently saw the L.70 go down in flames, and the L.63 made for home at speed. The L.56, also shaken by the sight of the flaming L.70, dropped her bombs in the sea off Lowestoft.

In all, 39 aeroplanes rose to intercept that night's raid. Of the night's losses on the defending side, two were naval aircraft—a Sopwith Camel from Burgh Castle, flown by Lieutenant G. F. Hodson, and a D.H. 9, also from Burgh Castle, with Captain B. G. Jardine and Lieutenant E. R. Munday aboard. It was thought that the pilots of these two aircraft, having seen the burning petrol from the L.70, mistook the patch for landing flares and crashed in the sea.

The L.70—Cadbury's victim—had been commissioned at Friedrichshafen as recently as July 8, 1918. She was just over 690 ft. long, had a diameter of 78 ft., a speed of just on 80 m.p.h., and a service ceiling of 23,000 ft. The L.70 had seven Maybach engines of 290 h.p. each. Her capacity was 2,196,900 cubic ft.

Mr. A Mattinson, of Saxmundham, told me: 'In the Great War the marker posts on Hickling Broad were replaced by buoys so that seaplanes could land there if the sea

Supermarine Southampton flying boats from Felixstowe visited Great Yarmouth in the late 1920s.

C. R. Temple

Joy flights from the old air station at Great Yarmouth in the 1920s. Picture shows an Avro 504K in flight with ships visible in background. *C. R. Temple*

at Great Yarmouth was too rough. I remember seeing a flying boat come over very low from the direction of Hickling, and we thought it must have got up from there, but it was the only one we ever saw which looked to have done so'.

Today Hickling Broad is a national nature reserve, owned by the Norfolk Naturalist Trust, and covers 1,300 acres. The 50 ft. high observation platform which I noted was there in 1970 was not a left-over from the flying boat days: it was intended for bird-watchers. All traces of the old hangars on the south denes at Great Yarmouth have gone, following industrial development, but in the 1950s the area was still largely undeveloped.

CHAPTER IV

East Anglian Aeroplane Makers

BOULTON AND PAUL LTD., of Norwich, who tackled aircraft production in the Great War, can trace the foundation of their business back to 1797, the founder being Alderman William Moore. Later John Hilling Barnard was taken on as a partner, and the business operated under the style of Moore and Barnard. Eventually, from these beginnings, Boulton and Paul came into being.

It was in 1915 that the Norwich firm started to make aircraft. Two years later the company was opening up an aeronautical experimental department. In the year that World War I ended, 1918, the company had started to construct all-metal aircraft. The Norwich firm in 1926 worked on the design and construction of the R101, the last great British airship. In August, 1936, aircraft production at Norwich finally ended with the transfer of plant to Wolverhampton, Staffordshire.

Within two years of the first aircraft order Boulton and Paul had an aeronautical experimental and design section at Mousehold, Norwich, where 'one of the largest aerodromes in the country' was available for test flights. Facilities, quite advanced for the time, included a four-foot wind tunnel, chemical and metallurgical laboratories, and physical testing machines for aircraft components. Extensive research was undertaken both into aerodynamical development and into the problems associated with the production of suitable steels for aircraft work and their protection against corrosion. It was in all-metal aircraft development, of which more later, that the company became especially noted.

How did Norwich become an aircraft production centre for something like 20 years? Well, when the government, soon after World War I started, were looking at likely centres they were drawn to Norwich because, quite apart from the necessary plant, Boulton and Paul had a nucleus of joiners and fitters.

In 1915 as already stated the company received its first order for aeroplanes: this was for a small trial order on a cost and profit basis for the manufacture of 25 F.E. 2b machines. Here it is interesting to recall that the first units completely equipped with F.E. 2bs, Nos. 20, 22, 23 and 25 Squadrons went to France in early 1916. They proved a match for the Fokker monoplane and in fact, on June 18, 1916, Max Immelmann, the most famous of the Fokker pilots, was shot down by a 25 Squadron F.E. 2b. The Norwich team, in order to glean knowledge of the production side, were promised the run of the Royal Aircraft Factory at Farnborough, Hampshire, but did not learn much.

Additional help at Norwich was enlisted from Mr. Stanley Howes of the coach building family. It was arranged that Boulton and Paul not only had the benefit of his services but the use of his Chapel Field works and men. At this time Captain J. J.

Dawson Paul was governing director of the company and Mr. Henry ffiske, who had joined the partnership in 1893, was managing director. Direct responsibility for initiating aircraft production fell to a large degree on two of the latter's sons, Mr. William·ffiske, who looked after the woodworking side of the business and its commercial affairs, and Mr. Geoffrey ffiske, who was most concerned, with Mr. Stanley Howes, with erection and assembly.

Construction of the first F.E. 2b began at the Rose Lane works, Norwich, the facilities of which were extended in 1916 by the opening of a new self contained factory at Riverside, Norwich, having its own railway sidings and river frontage and access by road to the cavalry drill ground at Mousehold. The fuselage of the first F.E. 2b (serial number 5201) was completed in the Rose Lane works and was moved to the Howes works at Chapel Field for the installation of the engine.

As the great day came round to demonstrate the first of the Norwich-built F.E. 2bs the War Office arranged to have a gala much sooner than the company felt was prudent. This meant that the machine went to Mousehold on October 1, 1915, to be rigged, necessitating men working all night on it. A big crowd assembled to watch the first flight but the F.E. 2b's 120 h.p. Beardmore engine would not start! But that fault had nothing to do with Boulton and Paul's handiwork: some engines, it appears, were not properly tested before delivery.

Apparently Lieutenant-General Sir David Henderson, one time Director of Military Training at the War Office, who was present with a large staff of officers from London, approached the aerodrome officer in charge who sent up all the machines he could muster in order to make up for the silent F.E.2b.

In his book, *Boulton and Paul and the Great War,* Mr. Henry ffiske said of that day of disappointment: 'Our poor old F.E. 2b was wheeled round for general inspection, the pilots and guests partaking of tea and light refreshment in a marquee provided for the purpose. Mr. Paul kindly bought up some magnums of "jump" wherewith to christen our offspring, and on being assured we could not be held responsible for what we call in Norfolk a "feeasso", allowed the bottles to be broached. It was subsequently found the magneto was at fault, and our first F.E. was in the air the following Monday . . . doing no less than 60 miles per hour'.

Mr. Stanley Howes, whose firm had joined forces with Boulton and Paul, volunteered to be their first civilian passenger when Captain C. Howard Pixton*, the well known pilot delivered their first F.E. 2b to Farnborough. On reaching Farnborough, Mr. Howes sent this telegram to Norwich: 'Arrived to schedule time, never want to travel motor car or train again, aeroplane every time'.

After that unfortunate christening Boulton and Paul never looked back—in fact, their work force of 1,800 men and women made 300 of the type, followed by a batch of 250 of the F.E. 2d type with the 250 h.p. Rolls-Royce Mk. I engine, the first bearing the serial number A6351.

---

*On April 20, 1914, he won the Schneider Trophy for Britain, presented in 1913 to the Aero Club of France by Jacques Schneider with the object of developing marine aircraft.

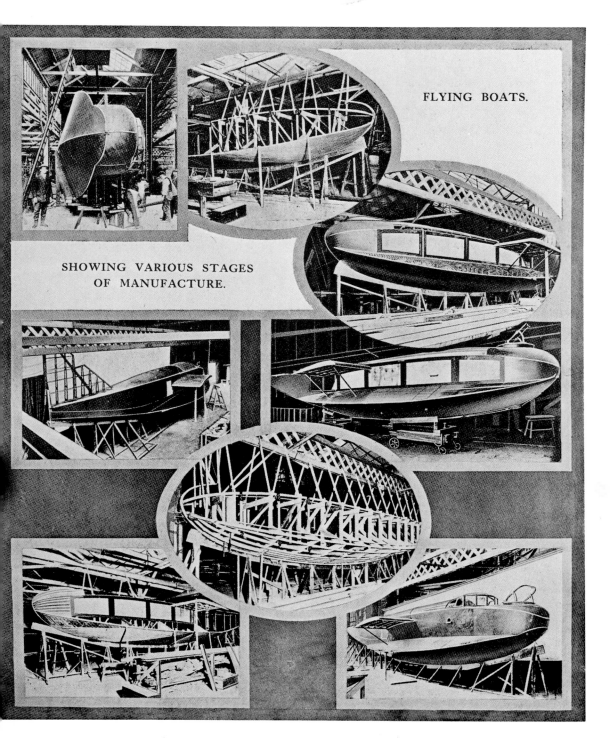

FLYING BOATS.

SHOWING VARIOUS STAGES
OF MANUFACTURE.

Boulton & Paul Ltd.

F.E.2ds produced by Boulton and Paul at Norwich in the First World War. The nacelles were by Richard Garrett & Sons Ltd., of Leiston.

Boulton & Paul Ltd.

The company, having had considerable experience as constructional engineers, also took on hangar production for the air arms and sent men to France to erect them. Aeroplane sheds were also erected by the company at such places as Felixstowe, Sedgeford, Narborough, Holt, Bacton, Covehithe and Aldeburgh. Some were sited in very exposed positions but withstood the blizzard of March 28, 1916, which was the worst for many years.

As Boulton and Paul learnt the techniques of aircraft production, and gained the trust of the War Office, they were asked to undertake wooden airscrew making, a very skilled job, as well. It seemed that as aircraft production increased in the country difficulties arose in finding experienced people to make airscrews, propeller making being the culmination of the woodworkers' craft on account of the accuracy of finish required. When the Great War came to an end Boulton and Paul had made a record number for East Anglia—7,835 propellers.

At the time Boulton and Paul were asked to take on propeller making 'this trade was confined to two or three makers' because the nature of the work required special experience. Later cabinet makers and carriage and motor body builders all over the country took up the challenge with remarkable success, it being recorded that Messrs. Watling and Sons, of Great Yarmouth, never had a propeller rejected. Interesting point about this firm, which had the benefit of local men released by Boulton and Paul, was that Mr. Ralph Watling was a maltster by trade and believed that 'a man could do anything if he would only educate and adapt himself to it'.

The extension to the works and consequent larger output of aircraft necessitated more room for erection at Mousehold. At the same time the question was being considered of 'making Norwich the acceptance park for the East of England'. An approach was made to Sir Eustace Gurney, as owner of the land on the Catton side of the Salhouse Road, with a view to putting additional buildings there, so as not to further reduce the flying ground. So it came about that this war time expansion set the pattern of what later became Norwich Airport.

After the company had proved itself in the production of F.E. 2 types—the total number produced was 550—further contracts were received, continuing through to the end of 1918.

First came a contract for 100 Sopwith Camels (starting with B5151). Other contracts followed at regular intervals to a total of 1,550 all of which were built at Norwich. At the peak in 1918 production was averaging 40 Camels a week, and when I visited Boulton and Paul in 1969 for the purpose of this section of the book, Mr. J. D. Paul, whose family played such a big part in the early growth of the company, showed me a photograph of a line up of no less than 43 Camels with, it was pointed out, four missing. So it seems that the company in one week—for the line up represented an average week's production—nearly topped 50.

Boulton and Paul, incidentally, built a number of Camels for the use of American pilots in the Great War. These were fitted with 150 h.p. Gnome Monosoupape engines.

D.H. 1A 4612 built by Savages Ltd. of King's Lynn.   *Edward Masterman*

The Boulton and Paul P.12 Bodmin J6910 of 1922. Designed as a transport the engines were mounted in the fuselage. By means of shafts and gears, they drove the four propellers. One other Bodmin was built and their main purpose was to investigate the possibilities of fuselage-mounted engines.

George Swain and Boulton & Paul Ltd.

Captain Frank T. Courtney, who went to Norwich in 1918 as air force test pilot, was given the job of testing the batch. As a freelance test pilot—Captain Courtney never joined the staff—his standard fee for three hours of test flying was £50.

Among strange features of the Mono Camel, as the type was called, was that the Monosoupape engine was 'throttled' by a selector switch which progressively cut out one cylinder only—with a noise exactly like the firing of a machine gun. Captain Courtney wrote in 1955: 'One day, having a lunch appointment at Harling Road, I turned up by diving on the hangars with the selector switch on "No. 1". There was a wild rush for shelter; and when I landed, expecting hearty laughter, I was nearly lynched. I hurried back to Norwich to tell *my* story to B. and P. before the official report got in'.

Camels caused 'many sensations in Norwich . . . being very quick on the turn and handy'. They were looped and spun with comparative ease and safety. Then followed contracts for the Snipe, which was an improvement on the Camel, the first being for a total of 400 aircraft (starting with E6137). It was the largest single contract placed with the company during the war period. Another 100 Snipes were ordered subsequently but not all had been built by November, 1918, and production was terminated a little short of the full total of 500 aircraft—about 425 in fact.

Very soon after their entry into aircraft production Boulton and Paul realised that they could not depend on sub-contractors for anything. A single bolt or odd size nut, if not to hand when needed, could hold up production for weeks. The company therefore went ahead and for some time made everything themselves, including eye bolts and ball races, in order to be independent.

Use of Boulton and Paul's woodworking experience was made by the establishment of a hull shop in which hulls for the big F.3 and F.5 flying boats were constructed. Before the company took on this new aircraft line, a team from Norwich visited Felixstowe to inspect a hull being built there under the supervision of Wing Commander John C. Porte, the flying boat pioneer, who took part in the inaugural raids of the R.N.A.S. against Bruges, Zeebrugge and Ostend. The team, it was recorded, were full of admiration for the very high class of work carried out there, but it was nevertheless felt that the wood craftsmen of Norwich could equal if not excel in such work.

An order for five hulls was offered to each of the contractors concerned, but Boulton and Paul turned it down as they considered that they would not be justified in 'disorganising' their workshops for an order of less than 30 hulls. The company,

A partly constructed Bodmin being moved to Mousehold for assembly.

George Swain and Bolton & Paul Ltd.

The all steel Boulton Paul P.15 bomber of 1923 with its metal skin removed.   *Boulton & Paul Ltd.*

full of confidence, pressed for 50 'on the understanding that if they were not satisfactory we should not be paid for them'. After Lieutenant-Commander Linton Hope, the well known yacht designer, had inspected the Norwich works, 30 hulls were ordered, and 10 keels worked on simultaneously. The first 10 hulls were finished in record time —in fact, it was said 'before any other contractor had delivered two'.

Boulton and Paul were invited with other concerns to quote for delivering hulls to Preston and South Shields. This was because they were too big to send by rail. Tanks were fitted at Preston, wings and engines at South Shields, and sometimes (presumably with wings folded) they were brought back to East Anglia—to Felixstowe —to be flown.

Boulton and Paul tried hard to convince the authorities that the Norfolk Broads and even Breydon Water were ideal havens for flying boats and, if utilized, would 'thus avoid the racket they were subjected to by the road journey'. In fact, in 1918, Captain Courtney, their test pilot, was asked to survey various possibilities for a site on the Norfolk Broads for their National Seaplane factory. As he had had little seaplane experience he went to the Great Yarmouth naval air station for tuition. But the National Seaplane factory project, which might have led to a second Felixstowe in the middle of Norfolk, was abandoned.

During the late 1920s Boulton and Paul developed the P.33 Partridge biplane. Dr. H. C. H. Townend evolved a means of cowling the radial engine which, with its large diameter, gave rise to considerable drag. The problem was to avoid impairing the cooling of the cylinders and this was effectively accomplished by Dr. Townend and the Department of Scientific and Industrial Research, in conjunction with Boulton and Paul, whose manufacturing facilities were employed to develop the Townend ring cowling. The ring, incidentally, was instrumental in increasing the speeds of aircraft fitted with it and was a popular device with designers for many years to improve the efficiency of their aircraft.

One of the company's most outstanding men was Mr. John D. North, who died in 1968 at the age of 75. Born in 1893, North, after a brief period as a student with Horatio Barber's Aeronautical Syndicate at Hendon, which is the site of the new R.A.F. Museum, became Claude Grahame-White's chief engineer. From the age of 20 onwards throughout his life he created a succession of aeroplanes of 'striking originality and great variety'.

The acceleration in all aeronautical work in World War I brought North further opportunities. In 1917 at the age of 24 he was appointed to the design side of Boulton and Paul where he accomplished his most mature work. His work ranged from light aircraft, such as the two seater Phoenix which was exhibited at the 1929 Aero Show at

Test pilot Frank T. Courtney (second left) with Boulton and Paul officials. Probably a P.15 Bolton bomber is being run up in background. *George Swain*

The 1927 Boulton Paul P.29 Sidestrand. Picture shows J9181 bomber. This type was supplied to 101 Squadron.

Boulton & Paul Ltd.

Olympia, to a highly original series of twin-engined aeroplanes for the Royal Air Force, among them, the Sidestrand and Overstrand of which the latter was equipped with the advanced Boulton and Paul mechanically operated gun turret.

The Overstrand, called after the Norfolk village of that name, occupies an important place in military aviation history. It was the first R.A.F. bomber—it appeared in 1934—to be equipped with an enclosed power operated turret. No. 101 Squadron was the only one to have Overstrands. Powered by two 580 h.p. Bristol Pegasus engines, the Overstrand had a top speed of 153 m.p.h., could carry a 1,600lb. bomb load, and had a crew of five. Although replaced as an operational bomber in 1937 by the Blenheim, the Overstrand was used as a gunnery trainer until 1941.

During an era in which the single engine biplane was almost uncontested among single seat fighters, North took a drastic step when he designed the Boulton and Paul P.31 Bittern, a twin engined monoplane which was a decade before its time in general design and in its special features. Appearing as far back as 1927, the machine was one of the earliest of single seat fighters with two engines and was intended for use against bomber formations. Two prototypes were built—J7936 and J7937. Instead of being fixed to fire forwards, J7937's pair of Lewis guns were mounted in barbettes on each side of the nose to incline from 0° to 45° in elevation, with the complete ring and bead gunsight hinged on a frame and connected to the guns so that it was elevated in concert with the guns. The entire armament system—it was too advanced for its time—could therefore be raised as a single unit to fire upwards at hostile aircraft.

Mann Egerton & Co. Ltd., of Norwich, having excellent coach-building facilities, were engaged in aircraft production in World War I, the 1914-1918 hangar still to be seen at the present Cromer Road premises being associated with that production.

Among the aircraft they built were Sopwith 1½ Strutters, Short 184 sea-planes, Short Bombers, Spad 7s, D.H. 10 Amiens, and D.H. 9s.

There is a photograph of Mann Egerton's Short Bomber 'N9490'. Mr. Bruce Robertson, aviation historian, told me: 'Mann Egerton built No. 9490 and not N9490 with which it was incorrectly marked. An official instruction at the time relates to the mismarking. This aircraft served with No. 4. Wing, bombing Bruges harbour on February 3, 1917.'

Mr. A. A. C. Jordan, of Aylsham, said in 1970 that he had tracings of general arrangement drawings of two experimental types which Mann Egerton, as far as was known, never developed beyond that stage. He said: 'One is for a seven seater touring type with two Rolls Royce Falcon engines, arranged in a central nacelle, push-pull, with the pilot in between. The passengers were to be carried in outboard nacelles. The other type is a two seater tractor biplane. It was to have had a 150 h.p. Hispano Suiza engine'.

In the Bridewell Museum, Norwich, which was formed to encourage the love of craftsmanship, there are a number of exhibits commemorating the city's link with aircraft production. There is a model of the first aeroplane, an F.E. 2b, which was

The 1927 Boulton Paul P.31 Bittern twin engined, single seater fighter. This picture of J7937 shows, front view, a pair of Lewis guns mounted in barbettes—a very advanced armament arrangement.
Boulton & Paul Ltd.

The 1929 Boulton Paul P.41 Phoenix light sporting aeroplane.   *George Swain*

built at Norwich in 1915. Then there are three relics—a wing, rudder and propeller—from the first all metal aircraft made in Britain and exhibited by Boulton and Paul at the Paris Aero show in 1919.

When Boulton and Paul were in full swing with the F.E.2b and 2d types, they were notified that they were to switch production to a single seater and, at the same time, give what assistance they could to Ransomes, Sims and Jefferies Ltd., of Ipswich, and Richard Garrett & Sons Ltd., of Leiston, in the production of a night bomber version of the out-of-date F.E. fighter. At the same time Messrs. F. Tibbenham, of Ipswich, tackled propeller making, and Reavell & Co. Ltd., also of Ipswich, handled contracts for 'gyroscopic sighting devices for bomb dropping from aeroplanes'.

Boulton and Paul assisted the Ipswich works considerably by building their new sheds for the F.E. programme. At the same time the Norwich company gave the run of their works to the Ipswich engineers, even to the extent of handing over templates and jigs and, what was more, the foreman of their fitter's shop.

Ransomes, Sims and Jefferies reached a maximum output of 60 F.Es a month. Their total aircraft production was 790. R. Garrett, starting rather late in the war, turned out over 200 F.E. 2bs. Four hundred D.H. 6s (C7201-7600) were also constructed at Ipswich.

Following publication of details about the destruction of the L.48 Zeppelin at Theberton in 1917, which is described later, Mr. Ernest E. Saunders, of Ipswich, said in 1951 that 'the biplane that brought down the Zeppelin was the F.E. 2b (serial number 401*), actually the first machine to be made in Ipswich'.

Mr. Saunders recalled that Ransomes, Sims and Jefferies had F. Tibbenham working with them making, in addition to the propellers already mentioned, wings, ailerons and tail planes. The 'White City' was set aside by Ransomes, Sims and Jefferies for aeroplane work, and the fuselage assembling and rigging was done by them, as well as the fitting of the Beardmore engine. When the first F. E. 2b was ready it was flown over Ipswich and was seen by the workmen at Portman Road skating rink, which had been taken over by F. Tibbenham. Alderman E. C. Ransome had the first flight. In 1917 the Air Ministry announced, and this is no doubt how Mr. Saunders was informed, that this first machine had been responsible for bringing down the Theberton Zeppelin.

As must have been the case all over the country, as firms geared themselves for aircraft production in the Great War, difficulties arose in the making of the first F.E. 2b at Ipswich. Practically all the wood working was done by hand as the machinery which was necessary for rapid production had not been installed. The 'doping' was done by men who had no knowledge of the fact that, with the room unheated except by slow combustion stoves installed temporarily to get the temperature up to somewhere near that required, there was danger of an explosion due to the gas from the paint.

*There now seems to be some doubt about Mr. Saunders' claim, repeated by the writer and others over the years. A letter was sent by the Commanding Officer of Orfordness Experimental Station to the Ipswich company in 1917. B401, it is agreed, was the Ipswich company's first F.E. 2b, but this one went to No. 37 Squadron. A 37 Squadron pilot was involved in the destruction of the L.48, but he was flying a B.E. 12 at the time. However, it is believed that B401 at some stage in its life took part in balloon barrage tests—possibly at Orfordness.

Boulton Paul P.29 Sidestrand. J9186 was a development machine and here shown with enclosed power operated turret, a feature of the 1934 P.75 Overstrand bomber of which J9186 was prototype.

Boulton & Paul Ltd.

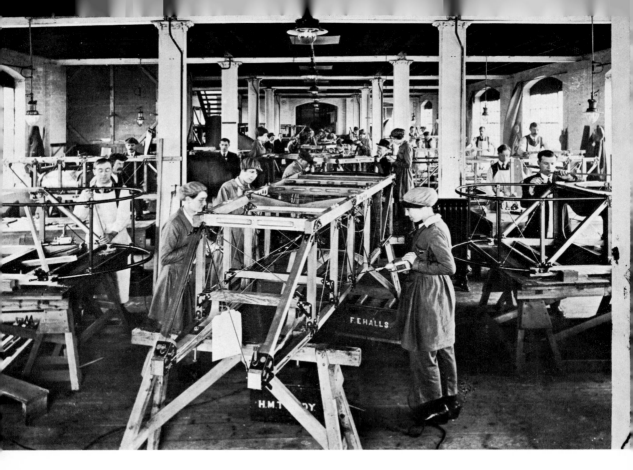

Aircraft production at Ipswich in First World War. *University of Reading, Ransomes Collection*

Parts for the first F.E. 2b took three months to make. However, towards the end of the war, no fewer than 20 sets a week were being produced by the Ipswich team.

The aircraft builders at Norwich, Ipswich and Leiston have already been described. At King's Lynn another company, Savages Ltd., whose St. Nicholas Iron Works were established in 1850, made their contribution to the air age in World War I. When Frederick Savage founded the company he was working in wood and iron, and we know that he used timber in the construction of wheels for his early traction engines from the year 1857.

Savages progressed from the repair of agricultural machinery to its manufacture, and then to the construction of fairground equipment. By the turn of the century the firm was known internationally for their engineered amusements. It was in the course of this work that Savages obtained the know-how which led to their aircraft interest, for did not metal, wood and fabric form the backbone of their fairground pieces?

Soon after the outbreak of World War I—it must have been some time between August and December, 1914—the late Mr. John Pilling, managing director, visited France. There he met M. Louis Blériot, the French aviation pioneer, who from his first big success in 1909, the Channel crossing, to August, 1914, constructed no fewer than 800 aircraft of 40 different types. Mr. Pilling returned to Norfolk with the manufacturing rights for the production of the Voisin Type LA biplane.

At the time of the order for 50 Voisin LAs the Aircraft Manufacturing Company at Hendon were engaged in the large scale production of Maurice Farman aircraft. A new two seat pusher aircraft, the D.H. 1, had also been built for the firm to the design of the British aircraft designer, Captain Geoffrey de Havilland. It was the first of the famous series. Lack of a suitable engine for the D.H.1 helped Savages to acquire yet another order. For the new aircraft has its first flight delayed until March, 1915, by which time the Hendon firm was committed on other aircraft. Thus the initial order was sublet to Savages. All but a few were of the D.H. 1A type with a 120 h.p.

First World War aircraft production at Ipswich included 400 D.H. 6s in addition to F.E.2 types.

University of Reading, Ransomes Collection

Short Bomber, incorrectly marked N9490 instead of 9490, by Mann Egerton & Co. Ltd., Norwich. A landplane adaptation of the Short 184 seaplane. *George Swain*

Beardmore engine fitted in place of the 90 h.p. Renault of the prototype. A metal tail replaced the earlier one which had a wooden frame.

In 1917 Savages received an order for D.H.6s—100 in all—and in the last year of the war an order for 100 Avro 504Ks, which ended the firm's aircraft interest. Altogether they turned out 100 D.H. 1s and 1As. All the aircraft made at King's Lynn were constructed on the spot with the exception of the engines. But in one or two cases the first Voisins were flown away from a field near the works.

Is there any evidence remaining today of Savages' contribution to the Allied air forces in World War I? It appears that the mainplanes fitted to the Avro 504K held by the Science Museum, London, were made at King's Lynn in 1918. Savages produced Avro 504Ks with the serial numbers E3051-3150 and the museum's example is E3104.

Sir Wilfrid Stokes, in a book called *A Short Record of the East Anglian Munitions Committee in The Great War* 1914-1918, pointed out that of the 42 Boards of Management throughout the country, East Anglia came third on the list for output, being only surpassed by London and Manchester.

East Anglia's World War I aircraft production has already been described. It seems, too, that the area might well have led the field in the production of aeroplane engines. When, in 1918, the Germans were pushing towards Paris, the output of aeroplane engines from the French factories was seriously menaced, and as the utmost capacity for manufacturing these engines in this country had been absorbed, an attempt was made to make them on a co-operative basis.

64

Various districts were approached—London, Scotland (including the Clyde), Manchester, Birmingham and East Anglia—and after very careful investigation 'the only contract placed for the manufacture of these engines on this basis was with the Board of Management of the East Anglian Munitions Committee'. However, owing to the Armistice in November, 1918, the contract was never completed.

Aylsham Road, Norwich in 1916 when Mann Egerton gave an air display at an Open Day. Fighter is a Sopwith Camel.   *George Swain*

CHAPTER V

The Growth of Martlesham Heath

FROM the early days of flying, except for World War II, Martlesham Heath, near Ipswich, which is now an industrial site, was the home of experimental units. It was formed as a fighter station in 1916 but in January, 1917 the Central Flying School Testing Squadron moved in and absorbed 'A' Flight of No. 37 Squadron which was already there. In October, 1918, the unit's title was changed to the Aeroplane Experimental Station and in 1920 to the Aeroplane Experimental Establishment. At about this time the question of moving the testing station from Martlesham was discussed, but there it remained and, in September, 1922, the existing experimental establishment was reorganised to include two squadrons of D.H. 9As. In March, 1924, Martlesham Heath became known as the Aeroplane and Armament Experimental Establishment, but when war broke out in 1939 the research facilities moved to Boscombe Down, Wiltshire.

It appears that Martlesham Heath was first officially mentioned in May, 1916, as on May 17 an interesting experiment was carried out from the already established R.N.A.S. station at Felixstowe. A large Porte flying boat, piloted by its designer, Squadron Commander John C. Porte, took off from Felixstowe carrying, strapped to its upper mainplane, a Bristol Scout (No. 3028), manned by Flight Lieutenant M. J. Day. When a height of 1,000 ft. had been reached over Harwich harbour the Scout pilot switched on his engine, released the clamps, and climbed safely away to land at Martlesham Heath. Not long after this Flight Lieutenant Day was killed in France. Mr. Gordon Kinsey, of Ipswich, who has made a special study of Martlesham Heath, told me in 1970: 'I think that this must be the first aircraft to use Martlesham Heath in an official capacity'.

At the end of 1916 the official testing ground for prototype aircraft was founded by Major Bertram Hopkinson, Professor of Engineering at Cambridge, who had been appointed Director of Aeronautical Equipment in November, 1915, at Martlesham Heath under the command of Lieutenant Colonel H. L. Cooper. The move from Upavon, Wiltshire, came about because the Central Flying School was expanding and the two roles were not compatible. Some months earlier—in June, 1916—the armament side at Upavon had come over to Orfordness for the same reason. Martlesham Heath grew up on part of the Pretyman estate.

Captain H. T. (later Sir Henry) Tizard, the scientist pilot, who was appointed technical officer, exerted a profound and lasting influence on British test flying. 'Soon', said Constance Babington Smith in *Testing Time,* 'under Tizard's lead, the very name "Martlesham" came to stand for everything that was most accurate and thorough in test flying. A Martlesham pilot was, by definition, one who could turn his hand to testing any variety of aeroplane and a Martlesham report meant a report that included an analysis of unprecedented detail and comprehensiveness'. Pilots who stood the course at Martlesham Heath for a number of years were 'absolutely first class'.

Proving of aircraft to 20,000 feet plus over the East Anglian countryside was a normal operating height after World War I. Open cockpits tried pilots to the full. Much of the earliest high altitude experimenting was, incidentally, done by Tizard himself. He came, in fact, to the borders of modern aviation medicine.

Another famous scientist pilot at Martlesham Heath was F. A. Lindemann, later Viscount Cherwell, who flew solo on November 9, 1916. There is an amusing story about him which relates how, while at Orfordness in 1917 testing the first stabilized bomb sights using live bombs, he dropped his precious stop watch through the floor of his aircraft. As, following the accident, Lindemann dropped no bombs, a colleague on the ground, who was to plot their fall, concluded that he had abandoned the test and went for a swim. Before landing Lindemann, for safety reasons, dropped the bombs, 20 pounders, in the sea. Later he learnt that they had straddled the bored plotter.'

In *The Prof. In Two Worlds,* the life of Viscount Cherwell, F. W. F. Smith said that Professor A. H. Gibson, who did engine research, remembered several strange characteristics in Lindemann. He, for example, did not like to appear conspicuous or unusual in his dress, flying kit being no exception. Professor Gibson recalled: 'He had to fly to Martlesham quite often from Farnborough. He would arrive at the airfield in bowler hat, long Melton Mowbray coat with velvet collar, and a rolled umbrella. Before boarding his plane which he piloted himself he carefully rolled up his coat, umbrella, etc., packed it under the seat and got into his flying kit. Before getting out of the plane at Martlesham he would reverse the process and would step out fully dressed in bowler hat, overcoat and umbrella. Of course the Martlesham pilots thought he was partially non-compos-mentis'.

In 1917, when Martlesham Heath took on experimental work, it was concerned with testing new military and civil aircraft before they entered service and, for some years, the activities of the station were confined to the testing of aircraft only. The armament section, as already mentioned, was the next stage in the development of Martlesham Heath, much of the work, including all the practical experiments, having been done at Orfordness on the Suffolk coast. There the section had the use of an airfield and special instruments for measuring results. Because of the nature of the work much of the experimental bombing was done by out of date aircraft.

Aircraft guns of all calibres were tested. Frequently it meant protracted flying trials at high altitude and extremely low temperatures. Lowest temperature recorded at Martlesham Heath was at 33,000 ft. when the pilot reported – 66° Centigrade or 119° of frost Fahrenheit.

Left. Lieutenant Colonel H. L. Cooper, the C.O. at Martlesham Heath in the early days. Right. Major Reginald H. Carr, test pilot at Martlesham in the First World War.   *Mrs Anne Hammond*

But a large number of the early pioneers have died. One of the outstanding pilots of the early days of Martlesham Heath—with his wife he paid a last visit to the aerodrome in 1967—was the late Major Reginald H. Carr who, I was interested to learn from Mrs. Gladys Carr, of Hendon, in 1970, started on his aviation career as mechanic to Grahame-White at Hendon in the very early days of British flying. Major Carr, who was born in 1886, was the son of Mr. Isaac Carr whose father, Mr. John Carr, had a shoe shop in the Thoroughfare, Woodbridge. To young Carr, when he was at Hendon, went the honour of being the first to loop-the-loop in an entirely British machine—a Grahame-White tractor biplane. Another milestone in his remarkable flying career was being pilot to William Newell on May 9, 1914, when over Hendon the latter became 'the first parachutist to make a successful descent from an aeroplane in England'. Carr took Newell aloft in a Grahame-White biplane for the historic drop.

What was Carr like in his early days? C. G. Grey*, writing about him in a programme for the autumn flying display in 1913, said he was short and wirily built, had plenty of stamina and wonderful strength for his size. He could see at that early

*Grey, former editor of the defunct weekly *The Aeroplane*, died in 1953 soon after arriving at a reception given at the Admiralty. As a journalist he expressed himself so boldly that he was perpetually in trouble of one kind or another. Advertisers became incensed when he attacked them and there were threats of libel action.

time that Carr was a pilot of 'very considerable ability' and a very fine engineer. Grey added: 'It was Reginald Carr who nursed the engines through all the big flights in America, when Mr. Grahame-White acquired sundry tens of thousands of good Yankee dollars'.

Mrs. Carr, in showing me notes left by Major Carr, turned up evidence that her husband, after a period of test flying at Martlesham Heath in World War I, was promoted and ran the flying side which flew every type, including captured German aircraft, that came their way. The fastest they flew in those days was about 125 m.p.h. Very few machines could go above 18,000 ft. but Major Carr, who must have found the experience exhausting, once climbed to 20,000 ft. in a Camel—without oxygen.

Martlesham Heath, of course, was responsible for the introduction of many outstanding inventions. For example, Major R. H. Mayo, well known as the designer of the composite aircraft, built a system at Martlesham Heath whereby an aeroplane could be flown by the feet alone so that the hands were left free to operate the gun, usually on a mounting above the pilot's head.

The first through flight from England to India was made by a four engined Handley Page V/1500 bomber from Martlesham Heath on December 13, 1918. The aircraft, which carried six men, was flown by Squadron Leader A. C. S. MacLaren and Lieutenant

Reginald Carr (left) and Claude Graham-White with whom he started his flying career as a mechanic.
Mrs Gladys Carr

Officers of the First World War photographed at Martlesham. Front row third from left is Major R. H. Mayo, designer of the composite craft. Captain J. Palethorpe, D.H.4 test pilot, is fifth with Captain (later Sir Henry) Tizard, the scientist pilot, next to him. *Mrs Gladys Carr*

R. Halley. Brigadier-General N. D. K. McEwen went as a passenger. Their Handley Page reached Delhi on January 16, 1919. The take off at 9.30 a.m. was watched by Mrs. MacLaren. It was noticed that, as the crew went aboard the giant machine, a small brown and white curly toy dog was perched on the hump of the fuselage. It was Squadron Leader MacLaren's mascot named after his pet dog Tiny.

A name associated with Martlesham Heath in the early 1920s was that of Harry W. 'Timber' Woods who was born at Great Yarmouth in the late 1800s. He was born next door in Nelson Road to James Sutton, coxswain of the local lifeboats from 1892 to 1902, and many times the boy Woods was left behind on the beach as the lifeboat made for a ship in distress. The excitement and challenge, no doubt, made an impression on young Woods and it found expression in the air—teaching men how to save themselves by parachute.

It was in the late 1930s that I first met Mr. Woods although he had been known to my family at Beccles, where he was married, for many more years before that. My meeting with him, as far as I can remember, came about because my brother became an apprentice in 1938 at No. 1 School of Technical Training, Halton, Buckinghamshire, not far from Mr. Woods' home at Aston Clinton. It was customary on parents' day for families to spend a day in the workshops, then full of World War I aeroplanes, and on the airfield which Mr. Woods' home overlooked.

I remember my first encounter, I was nine at the time, with the dapper little pilot. He produced one of his photo albums and very near the front was the photograph of his Westland Weasel machine on fire near Martlesham Heath on July 11, 1922—the day before his son Robert, who afterwards spent 27 years in the R.A.F., was born at Woodbridge. As I remember his version of the story, and he was not a man to exaggerate, he leapt out of the Weasel, without a parachute, and fell many feet.

Next day the *East Anglian Daily Times* had this to say about the incident: 'An exciting incident occurred on Tuesday afternoon near Martlesham Aerodrome. F/O Orlebar* and Sergeant Woods of the R.A.F. had been flying at a height of about 2,000 feet in a Westland Weasel machine, fitted with a Jupiter engine, when the machine caught fire. Fortunately a good landing was effected near the aerodrome, where the aeroplane came down safely to the ground. The occupants were soon liberated. Both were suffering from slight shock and burns, but neither was seriously hurt'.

The particular Weasel—No. J6577—was one of only four examples of that type. J6577 had several modifications, including a 400 h.p. Jupiter engine, and at the time of the accident was undergoing tests from the then Aeroplane Experimental Establishment for possible adoption by the R.A.F. as a fighter/reconnaissance machine. The type was completed towards the end of 1918 and had the unreliable ABC Dragonfly engine of 320 h.p. Two Vickers guns were provided for the pilot; the observer used a single Lewis gun on a Scarff ring. The four Weasels, though apparently 'quite successful' in flight trials, spent their flying life in an experimental capacity only.

Mr. Woods†, who died in 1967, first served with the Army as a gunner during the Great War, then joined the Royal Flying Corps while still on war service in Egypt. Later, when the R.F.C. and the Royal Naval Air Service became the R.A.F., Mr. Woods, by then a Flight Sergeant, started making parachute drops with Leslie Irvin's new free pack parachute.

Handley Page V/1500 heavy bomber with wing span of 126 feet at Martlesham Heath in 1919.

Mrs Anne Hammond

*Later commanded the High Speed Flight at Felixstowe.

†For a period in 1918 he was a pilot at the Observers' Training School, Aldeburgh, which used a landing area at Leiston. At the school Mr. Woods mostly flew D.H. 6s, and on September 23, 1918, he took up one Dowding. This officer became Air Chief Marshal Lord Dowding, G.C.B., G.C.V.O., C.M.G., victor in the Battle of Britain. Lord Dowding died in 1970 and on March 12 his burial took place in Westminster Abbey. Mr. Woods was awarded the A.F.M. for his parachuting exploits and piloting, which included twice bringing down planes with parachutists standing on the wing and unable to jump. He was awarded the M.B.E. after the last war for his work in the A.T.A.

Flight Sergeant H. W. Woods photographed when he was with the Air Transport Auxiliary in Second World War. Right, Wing Commander A. H. Orlebar. *Gordon Kinsey*

After a bad fall, which ended his parachuting career, he teamed up in 1926 with Corporal Arthur East*, aged 25, who was 'one of the R.A.F.'s bravest, most intrepid and most expert parachutists', to demonstrate parachutes all over the country, with himself piloting the platform, a Vickers Vimy such as Alcock and Brown used in 1919 for their first non-stop aerial crossing of the Atlantic.

Corporal East came to Martlesham Heath. Flight Sergeant Woods, who toured the country introducing the parachute to the R.A.F., (it became compulsory wear in 1925), was at the controls of Vimy No. F9161 on March 9, 1927, when Corporal East, before a crowd of service experts, fell to his death over Biggin Hill airfield, Kent. Shortly after this accident another member of the crack team, L. A. C. Ernest Dobbs†, aged 26, who had also jumped at Martlesham Heath but did not give his name to a local lane, lost his life on March 11 while carrying out private experiments in which he used a balloon for 'jumping over low hedges and trees'. L. A. C. Dobbs collided with 11,000 volt conductors carrying electricity from Willesden to Hendon.

Great Yarmouth's champion airman, before he left the R.A.F. to continue with Imperial Airways, took part in several of the famous Hendon air shows between the wars when, as leader of three Vimys, he would drop men, (two of the team were East and Dobbs), before crowds of 100,000 people. At his last Hendon display Flight Sergeant Woods, who spent 5,300 hours in the air, was called to the Royal enclosure to

*On September 29, 1926, from Vimy F9161 flown by Sergeant Woods, East did his first free fall over Duxford, the duration being 17 seconds before his parachute opened. It was 'the first fall of any appreciable duration made in this country'.

†The story is told that Dobbs was such a fearless parachutist that, on one occasion, he set out to prove that a badly packed parachute would open just as faithfully as a properly packed one. He 'bundled the large silk canopy and long lengths of shroud lines into the pack anyhow, pulled the sides of the pack over, slotted the pins, then went up and jumped. The chute opened instantly'.

explain to members of the Royal family some of the intricacies of the art of parachuting. It was a very proud moment for the Norfolk aviator.

The year 1922 saw the Martlesham Heath Air Ministry Competition for commercial aircraft. It was won by the Handley Page W.8. Afterwards Imperial Airways, partly as a result of the competition, adopted the type.

What was Martlesham Heath like in its heyday? Well, the best impression can be got from the 1938 programme: 'The station is divided into two main sections, the Performance Testing Section and the Armament Testing Section, both of which are under the command of the Station Headquarters whose offices are approximately in the centre of the Camp on the Woodbridge side of the Road. The Performance Testing Section consists of three Flights whose hangars are in a group at the end of the Aerodrome nearest to Woodbridge. The large green hangar houses the Flight which deals with the testing of large twin-engined aircraft, while the remaining two hangars at this end of the Camp house the two Flights which deal with small and medium sized single-engined aircraft.

'Proceeding along the main road through the Camp towards Felixstowe we come to the armament-testing hangars. The first one is mainly devoted to testing of guns.

Westland Weasel J6577 which, in 1922, landed in flames at Martlesham Heath. Orlebar and Woods survived the event. *Woods family*

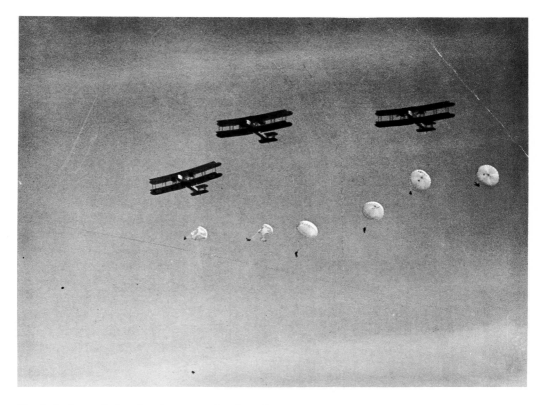

Woods leading a flight of Vickers Vimy bombers during a parachute dropping display at Hendon during the 1920s.   *Woods family*

Small and medium sized aircraft are employed for this work. The next hangar, the large green one in the centre of the Camp, deals with bombing tests, and contains a variety of aircraft mostly of large size. A further part of the Armament Testing Section is the armament work-shops which are situated on the side of the road opposite to the central hangars. Here also are the offices of the Stores and Accounts Section, the instrument shop, and the engine repair shop. Further along the road towards Felixstowe we come to the Aircraft Repair Section on the right, then the headquarters offices on the left, and finally at the far end of the Camp, we come to the barrack blocks for the airmen, the canteen, the airmen's dining room, and the sergeants' mess and officers' mess'.

An interesting machine—the Hawker Intermediate Fury G-ABSE—was one of a number of Fury variants tested at Martlesham Heath. A private venture of the Fury, it was an attempt to carry on biplane development in the single seat fighter interceptor field in order to assist in assessing the alterations proposed for a machine to be designed to Specification F.7/30. G-ABSE was flown by P. E. G. Sayer on April 13, 1932, and was extensively used for the next three years. The airframe was altered as tests progressed. Various engines were also fitted.

In 1933 the Bristol Aeroplane Company Ltd. turned its attention to civil aviation. A ten seater low wing all metal monoplane, quite revolutionary for the period, was designed. When finally produced—it was called Bristol Type 142 'Britain First'—it had seats for six passengers, was fitted with two Bristol Mercury engines, and was of all metal stressed skin construction. It was credited with 'a speed of more than 300 m.p.h.'.

When 'Britain First' was tested at Martlesham Heath for its Certificate of Airworthiness its performance so much impressed the Air Ministry that they asked to make further tests. The results were so outstanding and the official interest so great that the owner presented the aircraft to the nation. It was from 'Britain First' that the Bristol Company got the idea for the Blenheim bomber in 1936—the aircraft which within hours of war being declared flew against Hitler from bases in Suffolk.

Martlesham Heath, because of the nature of the experimental work carried out there, gave local people many a thrill. For instance, when Harald Penrose*, test pilot, who had Ipswich connections, was putting the Westland PV7 high wing monoplane through diving tests near Wickham Market on August 21, 1934, a wing fell off and

Left: Corporal A. East. Right, Leading Aircraftman E. Dobbs. *Woods family*

*Mr. Penrose, writing in the 1909-1969 Jubilee Supplement of *Flight International*, said he had flown over 400 widely different types and their variants in the course of some 5,000 hours, ranging from World War I machines down to ultra-lights with two-cylinder engines, and through four decades of development of military and civil aircraft into the jet-propelled age.

Aerial photograph of Martlesham Heath showing some of the main buildings.   *Gordon Kinsey*

dropped in Campsea Ash Park. The machine, when the wing struts failed, went into a dive and then a spin, but Penrose managed to escape out of the enclosed cockpit—the first such escape of its kind in this country. He came down by parachute near Blaxhall Hall. The main part of the aircraft, including the radial engine, plunged into the River Deben six miles away. The tail was found two miles from the wing.

Mr. Penrose, who now lives at Sherborne, Dorset, told me in 1970: 'My log for this incident merely states "Wing failed". While I was flying the PV7—it had no radio—a telegram arrived at Martlesham from Westland to the effect that speed must be limited to x m.p.h. with centre of gravity aft, the loading under test, as calculation showed an insufficient safety factor at terminal speed. The youthful me could not forebear replying, on returning to Martlesham: "Calculations absolutely correct. Congratulations" '. The test pilot's fortunate escape from an enclosed cockpit, incidentally, reassured R.A.F. pilots who previously doubted the feasibility.

Fighter aircraft like the Hawker Hurricane and the Supermarine Spitfire were all tested at Martlesham Heath before entering R.A.F. service. Thus Hurricane K5083, the prototype, after being flown for the first time at Brooklands on November 6, 1935, by Hawker's chief test pilot, Paul W. S. Bulman, who died in 1963, went in early 1936 to the Aircraft and Armament Experimental Establishment and by April of that year had been tested and reported on. Designed by the late Sydney Camm, the prototype reached a top speed of 315 m.p.h. in level flight at 16,200 feet. On June 3, 1936, Hawker Aircraft Ltd. received a contract for the production of 600 of the type,

Top: Hawker Intermediate Fury G-ABSE tested at Martlesham in 1932. Below: Westland P.V.7 high wing monoplane. *Ministry of Defence & Gordon Kinsey*

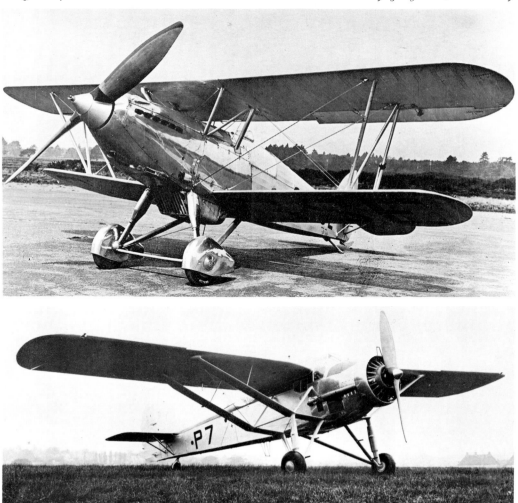

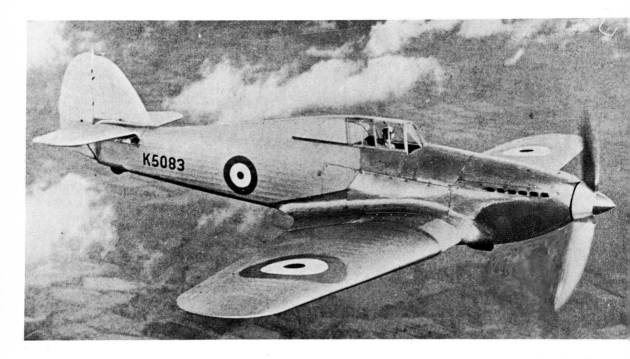

Hawker Hurricane K5083, prototype of the famous Battle of Britain fighter, went to Martlesham Heath for trials in 1936. *Hawker Aircraft Ltd.*

the name Hurricane being decided on on June 27, 1936. Two production models of the Hurricane were tested at Martlesham Heath between September, 1938, and January, 1939. Dive tests were carried out to 380 m.p.h. but it was noted that there was difficulty in opening the cockpit at that speed.

A few months after the prototype Hurricane had made its first flight the prototype Spitfire K5054, which was designed by the late Reginald Mitchell, who had earlier created the S.5 and S.6 Schneider Trophy seaplanes, first flew at Eastleigh, Hants., on March 5, 1936, in the hands of Captain J. Summers. It then went to Martlesham Heath. The first production order for the Spitfire—310 machines—was given on June 3 of that year. Mitchell, who had been in poor health while he designed the famous Spitfire, died on June 11, 1937, at the age of 42. A year later No. 19 Squadron at Duxford, Cambridgeshire, took the first Spitfires. The next squadron to take the Spitfire was No. 66, also at Duxford, which on July 11, 1940, while flying from Coltishall, near Norwich, fired the opening shots in the Battle of Britain.

In 1937 the famous Gloster Gladiator fighter biplane, the prototype was K5200, was tested at Martlesham. In the following year an advanced eight gun fighter, the Martin-Baker M.B.2, was tested at Martlesham but was not accepted by the R.A.F. It was P9594.

In the mid-1930s East Anglians had their first opportunity of attending Empire Air Day at certain airfields. The idea of holding an aviation 'At Home' and inviting all to come originated with the Air League of the British Empire. The League sought the co-operation of the Air Ministry, the flying clubs and aerodrome authorities, and in 1934, as the R.A.F. started to expand, Empire Air Day appeared in the aeronautical calendar for the first time.

I attended several displays at Martlesham Heath as a child and remember with what excitement the event was anticipated. The programme for Empire Air Day for May 28, 1938, is worth recalling. Synchronised aerobatics were carried out by two Hawker Fury fighter biplanes. An Avro Tutor, with instructor and pupil, demonstrated. Two Hawker Hurricanes, then a rare sight, approached from the Colchester direction and, as the leading pilot headed for Martlesham Heath, his reported progress was heard over the loudspeakers via the fighter's R/T. One of the Hurricanes was equipped for firing blank ammunition and most of the big crowd of spectators heard for the first time the sound of eight machine guns firing at once. Three Gloster Gladiators arrived tied together with tapes and, still tied, carried out clever formation stunts. A Westland

Major D. Geddes and friends set out in a Squadron car from Martlesham Heath during the First World War.
Mrs Anne Hammond

Lysander, then the latest Army Co-operation aircraft, showed its paces, the programme pointing out that 'with Handley Page slots along the whole of the leading edge of the wing . . . this monoplane can land slowly take off quickly, climb steeply and saunter slowly across the skies if its pilot wishes'. The pilot finished off the demonstration by picking up a message slung between two poles using a hook suspended beneath the Lysander.

One of the events most looked forward to was the annual battle involving tribesmen and R.A.F. aircraft, the programme explaining that 'The scene is an undeveloped country . . . under British protection'. The tribesmen, who were always well camouflaged, were hard to pick out across the expanse of Martlesham Heath, but their war like attitude, the programme stated, indicated 'that these tribesmen are backed by some foreign power since they are armed with modern weapons, including machine guns and gas bombs'. However, the small R.A.F. desert convoy under attack was saved by the timely arrival of three Vickers Wellesley bombers which put paid to the tribesmen. Then, with the tribesmen retiring in disorder, down came an ancient Vickers Valentia troop carrier with 21 troops to reinforce the position. Incidentally, the Valentia, which had two engines and a wing span of 87 feet 7 inches, sometimes carried a spare engine on the bottom inner port wing!

Another feature of the 1938 display at Martlesham Heath was the fly past of flying boats from the Marine Aircraft Experimental Establishment at Felixstowe—the parallel Establishment to the Aeroplane and Armament Experimental Establishment. Then, to round off the afternoon's programme, aircraft of greatly different speeds took part in a handicap race under Mr. F. Rowarth, official handicapper to the Royal Aero Club, who had for many years been responsible for the handicapping of the King's Cup Air Race. The aircraft did two circuits of a triangular course, each lap being about 18 miles, with turning points at Ipswich airport, Felixstowe air station, and Martlesham Heath.

I wonder what brought Service aviation to Martlesham Heath in the early part of this century? It seems to me that possibly a clue can be found in the following story related to me by Captain R. N. Phillips, veterinary surgeon, of Ipswich. 'I bought', he told me, 'the house and practice, at the corner of Handford Road and Cullingham Road, from a Mr. Roberts in 1947. The year of his death, his widow, who died in 1948, told me that a mechanic hired the garage for use commercially as a garage pre-1914 and on the door were the letters spelling garage cut out of one inch wood and screwed on. In this workshop was constructed the first aeroplane to be built in this district. It was taken out to Martlesham and there assembled for its first flight. But positive confirmation of this fact has yet to be established'.

What a splendid tribute it would be to those early pioneers of the air if a plaque or something of the kind could be placed on the site of the old airfield—before all evidence is swept away. Over at Cambridge, however, there is already a memorial to some of

1. Formation of biplanes over Aldeburgh in the First World War. 2. Sopwith Pup, piloted by Captain Vernon Brown, being looped in Aldeburgh area on September 6, 1917. 3. Handley Page 0/400 heavy bomber, wing span of 100 feet. Over Suffolk coast in the First World War on camouflage experiments.

Mrs Anne Hammond

Towards the end of the First World War Captain Roderic Hill deliberately flew an F.E. 2b into balloon cables at Orfordness. This was in order to see what protection aeroplanes needed against barrage balloons. Note wire fender on the F.E.2b which forms a ''V'' in front of the machine for this work,

Imperial War Museum

the Martlesham Heath breed. For on May 7, 1927, the late Air Marshal Sir John M. Salmond unveiled in the lecture hall of the Cambridge University Air Squadron an oak plaque inscribed with the names of three distinguished Cambridge scientists, Bertram Hopkinson, who founded Martlesham Heath, Keith Lucas and Edward Busk*, who lost their lives flying during World War I. Hopkinson, who was 40 when he learnt to fly, was killed while flying from Martlesham Heath to London. These men, the plaque notes, 'gave diligence, devotion, and life itself to the study of aeronautics'.

Round about Martlesham Heath, as if unable to leave their old roost, several survivors of the early days live on. For instance, at Thorpeness, near Leiston, two Martlesham Heath test pilots of the 1922-1926 period live. They are Air Vice Marshal John A. Gray and Air Commodore H. F. V. Battle. Then there is Group Captain C. F. H. Grace, of The Roundhouse, Martlesham, who was in command of the Parachute Section when it left Martlesham Heath for Henlow in the mid-1920s.

The present landlord of The Compasses at Holbrook, nr. Ipswich, Mr. Jack Easedown, was a test pilot at Martlesham Heath in the late 1920s, later flew for Hillman's Airways and as a test pilot again, for Handley Page. The founder of Hillman's Airways, the late Edward Hillman, who died in 1934, was one of the most remarkable personalities in road and air transport in Great Britain. After World War I he bought a motor coach and began a service in Essex between Romford and Clacton-on-Sea. He was so successful with coaches that he turned his attention to air transport and in November, 1931,

*In November, 1914, the B.E. 2c he was flying burst into flames and crashed near Laffan's Plain, Farnborough, killing him.

formed Hillman's Airways. His vigorous methods affected air travel in Great Britain in several ways. He made a considerable section of the travelling public airminded, and he asked the aircraft manufacturers to provide a passenger machine which could be flown at low running and maintenance costs. He expanded an air taxi business into an internal air line, and then decided to begin regular services to the continent. Mr. Easedown saw the growth of Hillman's Airways which in October, 1935, amalgamated with two other private airways to form British Airways.

Among the interesting interviews I had, while collecting information for this book, was with Mrs. C. Anne Hammond, aged 80, of Aldringham, near Leiston, whose late husband Captain W. Walden Hammond, the photographer, formed the photographic flight in the R.F.C. at Orfordness in 1916. This work also took him to nearby Martlesham Heath.

Mrs. Hammond made available to me two precious albums of unpublished photographs covering not only the service life at Orfordness and round about in World War I but the social life as well. It is to her, therefore, that the reader should be thankful for the rare aerobatic pictures and other shots in these pages.

Mrs. Hammond also made available the original day-to-day diary kept by her husband of photographic flights from Orfordness. Thus, for June 17, 1917, his twenty-second flight, when the great German Zeppelin L.48 crashed in flames at Theberton, not far from her present home, we find written evidence that Lieutenant Frank D. Holder, his pilot on many photographic flights, brought down, aided by his gunner, the L.48. We find the pilot and photographer circling over the burnt out skeleton of the L.48 a few hours later, at which time a number of photographs were taken of it.

1. Sopwith Triplane, probably N5430, at Orfordness. Flown operationally by naval units only.
2. Rare aerial view of airfield at Orfordness during First World War. Note canvas hangars and Bristol Scout. *Mrs Anne Hammond*

A number of captured German aircraft were test flown over Suffolk during the First World War. Top left is a close up of a D.F.W. C-V near Martlesham Heath. Right is a rare photograph of an Albatross D-V over river complex near Orfordness. Middle. Left is another picture of an Albatross D-V taken on September 24, 1917 again over Orfordness. Remaining pictures are of a Fokker E-III fighter.

Mrs Anne Hammond

Furthermore, Mrs. Hammond was able to tell me that, their work done, they did not celebrate in popular style, but went on Captain Hammond's sailing boat on the River Alde in the quiet of the evening, together, in remembrance of the fallen Zeppelin. Interesting, too, is the fact that a photograph was taken of Lieutenant Holder on the evening of June 17.

Captain Hammond's diary reference for June 17 noted: 'Pilot F. D. Holder—FE 2,000 ft. 35 mins.—flew over to take official records of the zepp Z48 brought down by Holder and his gunner a few hours earlier, i.e. 3.26 a.m.

'23rd flight: Pilot Capt. Wackett—FE 2,000 ft. 35 mins.—again flew over zepp for more photos.—fell asleep when returning'.

Captain Hammond's diary—he flew 112 times between March, 1917, and August, 1919—is full of interesting evidence of experiments at Orfordness. On March 30, 1917, he photographed Ranken darts being dropped. These steel incendiary darts, about the size of a large candle, were the invention of Engineer Commander F. Ranken, R.N., for use against airships.

For May 31, 1917, his seventeenth flight, Captain Hammond noted: 'Pilot Major Norman—FE 20 mins.—Holder had lost a wheel from his undercarriage so we took one up and flew alongside him—after chasing him for miles—and I held wheel up to warn him'.

For his thirtyeighth flight, on September 12, 1917, Captain Hammond was taken aloft in a BE2e flown by the scientist pilot F. A. Lindemann. Captain Hammond was the Very signaller in the leading aircraft of a formation of bombers. 'At the end', he noted, 'my fingers refused to pull the trigger. Coming down we stalled and stopped the prop so that we planed at gliding angle in perfect quiet and could talk easily'.

While night flying on November 5, 1917, in connection with vibration tests, the diarist noted that it was a 'very black night', the engine of their machine 'conked out' but Lieutenant Holder, Captain Hammond's favourite pilot, managed to scrape into the aerodrome. On February 23, 1918 the photographer got a bad fright when, having taken some air-to-air pictures of a Bristol M.1c., his pilot, Captain Haig, put the photographic aircraft without warning through some aerobatics, in cloud, without apparently knowing that Captain Hammond was not strapped in!

In the course of correspondence, before we met, Mrs. Hammond summed up their life at Orfordness and Martlesham Heath over 50 years ago: 'At one time the death roll was 100 per cent. per annum. The dear things would probably be dining with us one night and had "gone" the next night. Flying in those days was indeed a great risk, with such machines, doing aerobatics in the day, to test strain'.

Captain H. J. T. Saint, Martlesham Heath test pilot, with his gunner by a D.H.9 in the First World War.
Mrs Anne Hammond

Orfordness, which in later years was to see the birth of radar, was also the centre of important air experiments in World War I. Towards the end of the war a device was tried out at Orfordness for protecting aeroplanes against balloon barrages. The machine used for the tests was an F.E. 2b—a large biplane with a pusher propeller. It was fitted with a heavy 'bowsprit', and a fending off wire was stretched from wing tip to wing tip and across the point of the bowsprit. This formed a 'V' in front of the machine and the idea was that, if the machine ran into a balloon cable, the cable would be deflected (pushed aside) and the plane would continue on its way undamaged.

British pilots with a practical outlook suggested that the device might not work as well as the inventor thought. So a balloon was let up at Orfordness and Captain (later Sir Roderic) Hill, who did pioneer work on the inverted spin, took up the F.E. 2b and deliberately flew it into the cable. There was a long electric spark, the machine was retarded, and then went into a spin. The pilot, however, pulled the F.E. 2b out of the spin just before it struck the ground—and landed safely at Orfordness. The balloon cable had been successfully deflected, but it had cut into the leading edge of one of the wing tips, probably at a joint. Although the protective device was proved to be fairly successful by this risky test, it was never used on active service, but had the war continued it might have been adopted.

CHAPTER VI

Felixstowe and Mr. Churchill

FOR MOST of its long history the air station at Felixstowe, which did such splendid work between the wars as the Marine Aircraft Experimental Establishment, was associated with the development of seaplanes and marine craft, its opening date being August 5, 1913, when the first station commander was Wing Commander Charles E. Risk. However, the authorities must have had their eye on the area as a seaplane base some time before this because Lieutenant C. R. Samson, as he was then, who had a most distinguished record, first flew over Landguard Common on October 3, 1912, but it is thought that he was over the area in a Short S41 in June, 1912.

In the course of a local newspaper appeal for information about a reported descent in the sea of the First Lord of the Admiralty, Mr. Winston Churchill, while flying in the vicinity of Felixstowe before World War I, Mrs. Ivy Woollard, of Felixstowe, in recalling that Wing Commander Risk was her uncle, said that she collected Mr. Churchill's autograph on that day. Wing Commander Risk and other officers had their headquarters at the time at the Melrose Hotel, now the North Sea Hotel, Felixstowe, which in those days was run by Mrs. Woollard's parents, the late Mr. and Mrs. J. Butler. Mrs. Woollard added: 'My uncle brought Mr. Churchill to the Melrose Hotel to dry off and have tea. Mr. Churchill went back to London in my father's underwear'.

Before I detail Mr. Churchill's 'accident' to which Mrs. Woollard alludes, it is worth recalling that on an unknown date, presumably in 1913, Mr. Churchill, while flying as a passenger in a Borel monoplane, 'sideslipped into Harwich harbour from a height of 150 ft.'. The reason for the lack of information about this 'ducking' is that, right from the start of Mr. Churchill's interest in flying, there was a feeling that he was taking undue risks. In fact, he wrote fairly full letters about his early flying experiences, but kept off forced landings, which no doubt is the reason why the Borel story is lacking a precise date. But the second 'escape' made the local headlines in a big way and, what is more, it seems that, having changed to a new seaplane, trouble was experienced in restarting.

The forced landing which gave Mrs. Woollard the famous autograph occurred in a seaplane off Clacton on April 24, 1914, while the First Lord of the Admiralty was flying up from the Isle of Grain to inspect the Felixstowe base. It was reported that 'something went wrong with the engine, and the machine had to descend on the water close to Clacton jetty'. *The Times* next day adding: 'A mishap occurred to a seaplane piloted by Lieutenant J. Wilfrid Seddon, R. N., and containing the First Lord of the Admiralty as a passenger, at Clacton yesterday afternoon'.

While Lieutenant Seddon sent for another seaplane, Mr. Churchill walked to the Royal Hotel, where he remained unrecognised until a local journalist, who had been

Captain/Wing Commander Charles Risk (centre) with Lt. Charles Rathbone (left) and Lt. Eric Nanson.

Mrs I. Woollard

out in the Boer War, recognised him. It was while Mr. Churchill was on the jetty, before starting in the second machine, that he was approached by 'the local militant suffragists'. Suffragist literature was found in the first seaplane when the recovery party arrived. Replying to a question, Mr. Churchill said he considered it 'part of his duty to understand flying and to visit the great naval air stations'.

The Royal National Life-boat Institution featured in the Clacton incident, for *The Life-boat* for November 2, 1914, noted for April 24: 'At 8.25 p.m. . . . a request was made that the motor life-boat *Albert Edward* should be sent out to pick up the Government seaplane No. 79, and also a Government motor launch which had gone to her assistance, but had broken down . . . When the life-boat reached the motor boat both she and the seaplane were taken in tow and assisted to Harwich harbour . . .'.

On yet another occasion, it was in 1915, Mr. Churchill, from the Pier Hotel, Felixstowe, watched a flying display by seaplanes. Impressed by what he saw, Mr. Churchill requested a flight, and Wing Commander Risk was asked to take him up. While being moved over to collect the famous visitor, the seaplane 'dived and sank' and Mr. Churchill never got airborne.

Many famous names in the R.N.A.S. were associated with Felixstowe. Air Commodore Charles E. H. Rathborne, who was born in 1886 and later became commanding officer at Felixstowe, was at the Suffolk base as early as 1914 when he went to France. It was while serving over there that he was shot down and taken prisoner. He was one of 29 prisoners who escaped from Holzminden camp by means of a tunnel in July, 1918. Rathborne, who spoke fluent German, reached Holland where he sent the following postcard to the German camp commandant: 'Thanks for the holiday. See you after the war'.

Another Felixstowe figure was Captain Henri C. Biard who died in 1966 at the age of 74. The captain, who started flying in 1910, established the world air speed record of 145.7 m.p.h. in 1922. Author of *Wings,* Biard, who in later years was chief test pilot for Vickers Supermarine, was a visionary and predicted many of today's aeronautical developments, including space travel.

Then there was Lieutenant Colonel C. R. Finch-Noyes, who invented a much needed incendiary bomb in the first year of World War I. In private life he was author and playwright, his early achievements in this sphere being *The Hornet* and the patriotic play *The Bull Dog Breed.*

Another Felixstowe pioneer was Commander C. R. Samson who, it will be remembered, flew over Landguard Common as early as 1912. In December, 1914, Samson led a night flying raid on Brussels, and in February, 1915, was in command of 34 landplanes and seaplanes in an attack on the Belgian coast.

How did the Felixstowe line of flying boats come about? The H.12 Large America flying boat, which was a development of the Curtiss Small America class, was the true forerunner of all later World War I British flying boats. H.12s of the 1910 period were fitted with two 275 h.p. Rolls-Royce Eagle I engines. The hull of the H.12 was covered partly in plywood and partly in fabric and it could not operate from rough water without risk of damage to the hull. Yet this type of flying boat carried out valuable North Sea patrols from Felixstowe and Great Yarmouth in the hands of resolute airmen. The H.12 was superseded by the F. (Felixstowe) series of flying boats, the F.1, F.2 and F.3. Wing Commander John C. Porte, who helped Boulton and Paul at Norwich when they took up flying boat production in World War I was primarily responsible for these developments, having already played a part in the design of the original H.12

A Borel seaplane being prepared for flight at Felixstowe.   *G. F. Cordy*

1) Short seaplane No. 79, which made a forced landing at Clacton on April 24, 1914, with Winston Churchill aboard, awaiting a tow. 2) Short seaplane No. 19 sent from Felixstowe to Clacton when No. 79 was forced down by engine trouble.   *W. Cross and Suffolk Photo Survey*

in America. All the F. series of flying boats were tractor biplanes. It is true to say that the F.2A and the F.3 bore the brunt of the North Sea air war effort after the H.12.

'In this work', noted C. F. Snowden Gamble in his book *The Story of a North Sea Air Station,* 'Wing Commander Porte and his staff at Felixstowe air station must be remembered always. Wing Commander Porte, though suffering from tuberculosis of the lungs, devoted all the energy of which he was capable to the successful production of flying boats'. Of him—he died in 1919 at the age of 36—the first official historian of the R.A.F., the late Sir Walter Raleigh, said: 'The shortest possible list of those who served the country in its hour of need would have to include his name'.

An interesting feature peculiar in aviation to some of the big twin-engined Felixstowe and Great Yarmouth flying boats of the closing years of World War I was the introduction of dazzle painting. Dazzle painting was the idea of Norman Wilkinson, the marine artist, for the camouflaging of merchant ships. The special dazzle painting for each ship was designed so to distort her outlines as to make her appear to be moving on a course other than that which she was following. This use of dazzle painting on flying boats, incidentally, was the only application of the artist's scheme to aircraft.

Then, on July 22, 1917, Harwich, which was an important naval base, was attacked in daylight by 15 Gothas. The formation crossed the Suffolk coast at Hollesley Bay. As the raiders turned south they dropped 55 bombs between Bawdsey and Harwich. Thirteen people—mostly servicemen—were killed and 26 injured.

The final score against the Zeppelins fell to offensive aeroplanes working with the navy. Lighters, towed by destroyers, were taken across the North Sea to engage enemy aircraft in home waters. The practicability of the scheme, which involved some risk to the pilot, was demonstrated at Felixstowe towards the end of July, 1918, when Lieutenant Stuart D. Culley successfully rose in a Sopwith Camel from a towed lighter.

Not many days later, on August 11, during an operation by the Harwich force off the Frisian coast, Culley in a Camel flying from a lighter shot down the L.53 near Borkum Riff lightship to the north of the island of Ameland. Culley's success, he was in the water for two hours, was described as 'an outstanding achievement second to none of the many glorious records of the R.A.F.'. Culley, in reporting what he saw of the L.53's last moments, believed that a crew member, his clothes on fire, dropped three and a half miles into the sea without a parachute. The German was apparently picked up, practically unhurt, by a Dutch fishing vessel, but from a medical standpoint this is said to be unlikely.

Behind this success lay other experiments in which great risks were taken, the proposal to use lighters for releasing flying boats at sea being first made in 1916. Then, in February, 1917, the first trials were made off Calshot, near Southampton, followed by experiments from Felixstowe on September 3, 1917. On May 30, 1918, using a landplane, a Camel, a test was made off Orfordness with a lighter towed by the destroyer *Truculent*. Watching the Camel experiment was Lieutenant Colonel E. D. M. Robertson, the then commanding officer at Felixstowe, and what he saw was absorbing. For the Camel, with Lieutenant Colonel C. R. Samson at the controls, failed to lift properly, even when the destroyer opened up to 32 knots, and plunged over the bow of the lighter so that it was literally run over. Wreckage bobbed up a long way behind the speeding destroyer and then, to the relief of the watchers, an exhausted but otherwise cheerful pilot.

No. 230 Squadron, which was formed in the autumn of 1918 from the anti-submarine patrol unit at Felixstowe, may be said to have inherited in part the tradition of that famous East Coast air base. In May, 1922, however, the squadron moved to Calshot

The late Wing Commander John C. Porte. *East Anglian Daily Times*

on Southampton Water and was disbanded a year later. Then the squadron was reformed in 1934.

In 1919 a flight was made by a British flying boat to demonstrate the commercial possibilities of the F.5 in Norway. Two flying boats left Felixstowe and flew to Dundee before setting course for Norway. They encountered driving rain and dense fog, which thickened off the Norwegian coast. One of the machines was forced back to Dundee, but the F.5 (N4044), flown by Major J. Galpin and Captain C. Scott, went below the fogbank and reached Kristiansand, the landfall being within two miles of the spot intended. This flight of 430 sea miles in seven and a quarter hours in bad weather was considered a remarkable example of navigation in those days. After a tour of Scandinavia the F.5 returned to Felixstowe, having flown 2,450 sea miles in about 40 hours' flying time.

Not only were British built flying boats tested at Felixstowe between the wars but many foreign types as well. For example, two Rohrbach IIIA flying boats of German design were tested there in the mid-1920s. It appears that a sister company of the Rohrbach Metallflugzeugbau, Berlin, was established in Copenhagen under the name of

Rohrbach Metal Aeroplan Companie during the period when Germany was forbidden by the Treaty of Versailles to build large aircraft. The parts for the two flying boats were made secretly in Berlin and sent to Denmark, where the aircraft were assembled and tested. The pair were bought officially by the British government which, it will be remembered, had signed the treaty forbidding the building of such aircraft in Germany. In the end both flying boats—they were of metal construction—were scrapped.

Felixstowe had its share of crashes with loss of life. For example, on April 29, 1920, the F.5 flying boat (N4044), which flew to Norway in 1919, while on an instructional flight coming from the direction of Manningtree, went into a fatal spin. A desperate effort was made by the pilot to pull it out of the spin and, if there had been another hundred or so feet to spare, it would have succeeded. What happened was that the flying boat hit the water as it pulled out of the swoop and was smashed to pieces. Of the crew of six four died and two survived. The dead included Squadron Leader Edwin R. Moon and Flight Lieutenant Albert J. Fyfield. When the funeral took place Squadron Leader Moon, who was well known at Felixstowe, was remembered with

A Short Sunderland flying boat moored at Felixstowe. Jetty was a refuelling pier. *Allan Jobson*

many floral tributes from local people and 'the flight mechanics and engineers, and the corporals and airmen at the station'. It was pointed out at the time that the squadron leader had a year earlier survived when the ill fated Felixstowe Fury crashed in Harwich harbour.

When Felixstowe air station was opened in the summer of 1913 it consisted of three sheds and a wooden slipway. The River Orwell, flowing up to Ipswich, was the anchorage.

Established in 1924, the Marine Aircraft Experimental Establishment, Felixstowe, in partnership with landplane establishments like Martlesham Heath, had several functions to perform. It served as an independent assessor of new aircraft, testing for the Royal Navy, the R.A.F. and the civil side. In this capacity it provided estimates of performance and assessments of handling qualities before aircraft were officially accepted for service. A second function was the collection of information on new trends in flying boat design and on improvement to existing designs obtained from research and development tests on full scale and model seaplanes. Besides these two primary duties connected primarily with seaplane design, the Felixstowe establishment also tested such equipment as marine craft which served as refuellers and as safety and fire fighting craft.

As Felixstowe developed more spacious hangars were erected. The crane pier was completed in 1932, and two years later the 50-ton Titan crane, a landmark for miles around, was put in.

Felixstowe's most famous unit was the High Speed Flight which flew the famous breed of Supermarine floatplanes, the Flight in the first year of its formation winning the Schneider Trophy for Great Britain in 1927 and again in 1929 and 1931. In the latter year Britain won the trophy permanently. It was a great technical victory, with the speed record of 340.08 m.p.h. of secondary importance, for it led directly through a line of high speed planes to the development of the Supermarine Spitfire fighter powered by the Rolls-Royce Merlin engine—the end product of co-operation between the Rolls-Royce Company and the Supermarine Company. The Schneider Trophy, a large silver trophy, had been presented as far back as 1913 to the Aero Club of France by Jacques Schneider with the object of developing marine aircraft.

However, it was not until the mid-1920s that Britain started to appreciate that the Schneider Trophy contests meant more than the mere adding of a few miles an hour to an annual record. The High Speed Flight had its first headquarters at Felixstowe and was formed as part of the R.A.F. Gloster machines were used for practice for the 1927 bid, six high performance float-planes being ordered for the race by the British government, of which three, the maximum number from any one country, were allowed to compete. The pilots were Flight Lieutenant A. M. Webster, who helped to run the old Suffolk Aero Club and later retired as an Air Vice-Marshal, flying a Super-

1) Felixstowe Fury, powered by five 334 h.p. Rolls Royce Eagle VII engines. 2) Curtiss H.12 Large American flying boat. 3) Back left is a Felixstowe F.2a. Centre is Felixstowe Fury. Back right is the Porte Victoria P.V.9.

Imperial War Museum and Bruce Robertson

Supermarine S.6B S1596 in which Ft. Lt. John Boothman won the Schneider Trophy outright at a speed of 340.08 m.p.h.

Ministry of Defence

marine S.5 with a geared propeller; Flight Lieutenant E. N. D. Worsley, flying another Supermarine S.5 but with a straight drive, and Flight Lieutenant S. M. Kinkhead, who lost his life in 1928 and is buried at Fawley, near Southampton, flying a Gloster IVB. Flight Lieutenant Webster was the victor at a speed of 281.68 m.p.h.

After the 1927 race the High Speed Flight, which had brought such honour to the R.A.F., was more or less disbanded, but it was reformed at Felixstowe in 1929 under Wing Commander A. H. Orlebar with the following pilots: Flight Lieutenant D. D'Arcy A. Greig, Flight Lieutenant G. H. Stainforth, Flying Officer R. L. R. Atcherley* and Flying Officer H. R. D. Waghorn. Flying Officer T. H. Moon, who worked with the team in 1927, was included as engineer.

The work of the High Speed Flight reached a climax in 1931, when it had to fly for the right to retain the Schneider Trophy permanently for Britain, the rules of the contest making it necessary for a country to win the trophy three times in succession in order to keep it. Again commanded by Wing Commander Orlebar, the team was made up of Flight Lieutenant Stainforth, Flight Lieutenant J. M. Boothman†, Flight Lieutenant F. M. Long, Flight Lieutenant E. J. L. Hope and Flying Officer L. S. Snaith. They were joined later by Lieutenant G. L. Brinton, R.N., who was killed on August 18, 1931, during a test flight in Supermarine S.6 (N247). On September 13 Flight Lieutenant Boothman, at a speed of 340.08 m.p.h., won the trophy outright. The final test on his winning machine, Supermarine S.6B (S1596), had a few hours before been made by Flight Lieutenant Long who was the son of the Rev. F. P. Long of Wells-next-the-Sea on the north Norfolk coast. The Norfolk pilot, he was 31, had been adjutant at

*Air Marshal Sir Richard Atcherley, K.B.E., C.B., A.F.C., one of the most striking personalities the R.A.F. has produced, died, aged 66, in 1970.

†The winning pilot in 1931, he served with distinction in the R.A.F. until his retirement in 1956 as Air Chief Marshal Sir John Boothman, K.B.E., C.B., D.F.C., A.F.C., Air Officer Commanding-in-Chief, Coastal Command. He died, aged 56, a year later. Apparently, when he was 10, Boothman was taken for a flight by the celebrated 'Colonel' Cody —an experience he never forgot.

Felixstowe. A fortnight later Flight Lieutenant Stainforth set up a new world speed record of 407.5 m.p.h. in the same S.6, a record which was to remain for two years until Italy captured the speed record for seaplanes.

Between August 12 and September 11, 1927, four machines belonging to the Flying Boat Development Flight, Felixstowe—Blackburn Iris II, Saunders Valkyrie, Short Singapore and Supermarine Southampton—did a flight to the Baltic and back to their Suffolk station. They were led by Squadron Leader C. L. Scott, and Sir Samuel Hoare, then Secretary of State for Air, accompanied the flight to Copenhagen. The distance covered was about 9,400 miles.

In the same year, on October 17, four Supermarine Southampton flying boats set out from Felixstowe on the longest formation cruise of flying boats in the world. Led by Group Captain H. M. Cave-Brown-Cave, whose brother, Wing Commander Thomas R. Cave-Brown-Cave, was an airship expert and was known at Pulham, the team of 16 men flew to the Far East and Australia, a distance of 24,000 sea miles, during which the unit was self-contained. They never made the hop back to this country because the Special Flight was renamed No. 205 Squadron with Seletar, Singapore, as its base, the end of the formation cruise being September 15, 1928.

Other flying boat cruises followed from Felixstowe. Between October 7-14, 1929, two Supermarine Southamptons, led by Squadron Leader C. Scott, flew to Norway and back. Two Short Singapores of the Flying Boat Development Flight between August 15 and September, 1931, cruised to the Middle East and back, their pilots being Flight Lieutenant H. Davies and Flight Lieutenant C. H. Cahill. They covered over 6,500 miles. In 1932, between September 5-24, a Supermarine Southampton of No. 210 Squadron, commanded by Wing Commander R. Leckie, who

Remarkable 'air display' off Felixstowe concocted by the celebrated local photographer, Mr. Emeny.
F. Hussey

took part in the shooting down off the Norfolk coast in 1918 of the L.70, visited a number of Baltic ports in the course of a 2,800 mile cruise.

Among other well known names associated with Felixstowe, including Flying Officer (now Sir) Frank Whittle, British inventor of the jet engine, who was there in 1932—1933 was No. 352087 Aircraftman John H. Ross (later known as No. 338171 Aircraftman T. E. Shaw), better known as Lawrence of Arabia, who enlisted in the R.A.F. in 1922. Together with a Corporal W. Bradbury, Aircraftman Shaw helped to advise, test and report on the various types of marine craft produced for the R.A.F. at Hythe, Kent. Co-operating with Bradbury, the famous Shaw was responsible for writing the original notes on *The 200 Class R.A.F. Seaplane Tender* for the R.A.F. Marine Branch.

On April 21, 1933, it was officially decided that Aircraftman Shaw 'is to be posted to Felixstowe for employment in work which is done there in Marine Craft section . . . he will be attached to contractors' yards. To avoid publicity he should wear plain clothes'. So Aircraftman Shaw alias Lawrence of Arabia, man of many sides, was able to get on with one of the jobs he cared most about—the development of high speed marine craft.

Aircraftman Shaw brought with him to Felixstowe his personal speedboat named *The Biscuit*. It had been presented to him by Major Colin Cooper, an American.

Felixstowe built up great knowledge of flying boats and their construction. Then, in the early 1930s, it became clear that the air routes of the British Empire, with their long transoceanic and transcontinental crossings, required aircraft of exceptional performance. Short Brothers Ltd., of Rochester, Kent, therefore designed and built the Short Empire series based on the many years of experience gained by Imperial Airways flying to schedule on these routes with other types of aircraft. The Empire series, the boats were all metal, represented many departures from orthodox practice.

So it came about on February 21, 1937, that one of the new boats, the 'Cambria', made a flight round Britain and was seen off Great Yarmouth with Captain G. J. Powell at the controls. Next day's *Eastern Daily Press* had this to say: 'Even though we are rapidly getting used to spectacular achievements in flight there is something about these striking times of the new flying boats that takes the breath away'. The 'Cambria', in the space of eight hours, flew a distance of some 1,400 to 1,500 miles and still found time to spare a few minutes over a number of towns. The *Eastern Daily Press* went on to comment that 'the most startling thing about this latest flight is that within five minutes of finishing her circuit over Colchester the 'Cambria' was seen from Yarmouth'.

I did not see the 'Cambria'. However, later in 1937, on August 30, I was taken at the age of eight to Pakefield cliffs to watch a sister "Empire" boat, the 'Caledonia', go by with Captain A. S. Wilcockson at the controls. He was on a round Britain flight, taking in 66 different coastal towns, and he had set out from Hythe, Kent. My first

1

3

2

1) Supermarine Sheldrake flying boat of 1928 in flight near Felixstowe .2) The Short Mayo **composite** or pick-a-back aircraft designed by Major R. H. Mayo. 3) Supermarine Air Yacht designed by R. **Mitchell** and built for private use by Hon. A. E. Guinness.   *Imperial War Museum, Short Bros. Ltd. and*
F. Hussey

In 1932-1933 Lawrence of Arabia, here in his speedboat, *The Biscuit*, served in the R.A.F. at Felixstowe.

R. Forbes-Morgan

impression of the flying boat, which had a wing span of 114 feet and a length of 88 feet, was that she looked like a dragon as she swept round Covehithe Ness and headed for Pakefield, flying below the cliffs in places. Next day the *Eastern Daily Press* had this to say about the flight: " 'Caledonia' zooms round the coast to remind us who stay at home that we have machines of such precision, speed, and endurance that we shall soon be making week-end trips to the New World, spending Bank Holidays in the Indies and Christmas in far Cathay". In that edition of the paper the 'Caledonia', having flashed past Pakefield, was pictured passing over Cromer Pier where she created "intense interest".

Incidentally, in 1937, too, the 'Caledonia', with the 'Cambria', carried out survey flights for the projected regular service between Great Britain and the United States. For example, in a maiden flight from Foynes, Iceland, the 'Caledonia' reached New-foundland in 15 hours three minutes, averaging 132 m.p.h., and did the return journey in the fast time of 12 hours seven minutes, averaging 166 m.p.h. By the end of 1937 28 Empire class flying boats were with Imperial Airways. With 24 passengers aboard, plus a load of mail, they could 'unstick' (leave the water) in a run lasting only 21 seconds. They were in all respects the culmination of years of research, much of which was undertaken at Felixstowe.

However, the Short Empire flying boats, although excellent for the shorter runs to Africa and India, could not cope with the Atlantic, and even the improved C class, which came to Felixstowe, were not good enough. It was then that the idea of refuelling in flight was born. A Handley Page Harrow acted as a tanker, transferring 7,000 lb. of fuel by hose to the flying boat. There were, however, drawbacks to this method.

Felixstowe then saw experiments with the Short Mayo composite or pick-a-back aircraft, the mother seaplane—a Short Empire type—carrying aloft a smaller seaplane. The mother seaplane was named 'Maia' and the smaller seaplane, whose engines helped the larger craft to take off, was named 'Mercury', the designer being Major R. H. Mayo, one of the early Martlesham Heath test pilots. On reaching a safe height the 'Mercury' with a full load of fuel was released and continued across the Atlantic with its cargo. This method was not particularly economical either.

The famous Short Sunderland flying boat of the war years, which played a vital part in the battle of the Atlantic and the U-boat war, was a military development of the Empire class. On April 21, 1938, Sunderland L2158, the first of the original seven production models to be finished at Rochester, was tested and in May was delivered to the Marine Aircraft Establishment, Felixstowe, for further testing. The second machine in the batch, L2159, was flown by a No. 210 Squadron crew from Felixstowe to Pembroke Dock, Pembrokeshire, on May 28, 1938—Empire Air Day.

In 1957, while visiting Felixstowe Ferry, I discovered a number of flying boat hulls being used as house boats and stores. Two of the hulls were positively identified as having come from the nearby seaplane base. One hull of wood, which was a relic

Hull of 1925 Supermarine Southampton, left, used as a house boat at Felixstowe Ferry, was moved, in 1967, to the R.A.F. Museum at Hendon. The hull of the Fairey Atalanta, right, was also used as a house boat but was finally broken up and burnt. *Author*

from a 1925 Supermarine Southampton flying boat, was 10 years later recovered for preservation in the R.A.F. Museum at Hendon. Later Southampton hulls were of metal.

The most interesting hull, however, was that bearing the name 'Atalanta' on its nose. Mr. Owen Thetford, who has written several books about aircraft, commented at the time: 'Your discovery at Felixstowe is interesting . . . The 'Atalanta' was designed to an Admiralty requirement in 1918 and only made its first flight on July 4, 1923. It was one of the only two flying-boats ever to see the light of day from the Fairey Aviation Co. Ltd., they designed a third which, however, was not built, the other being the 'Titania' . . . The aerostructure of the 'Atalanta' was designed by the Fairey concern, but the hull was by Linton Hope. It was. built by a firm called Dick Kerr, the hull being supplied by May, Harden & May'.

Mr. Bruce Robertson, who for many years has been researching into aircraft histories, added his piece in 1957: 'As the 'Atalanta's' hull probably travelled more miles by road than it did in the air, its itinerary may be of some background interest. May, Harden & May had a boatyard at Hampton Wick, Middlesex, and premises on the south coast. I imagine that the hull was built at the latter place. It was transported by road from the south to Dick Kerr's works at Lytham-St. Anne's, Lancashire, via Wales, to avoid narrow streets and obstructions, such as trams, in some Midland towns. The superstructure was built at Lytham-St. Anne's and the boat was erected, dismantled and conveyed to the Isle of Grain, Kent, for testing, later moving to Felixstowe (the Marine Aircraft Experimental Establishment moved early in 1924 from Grain to Felixstowe) where it was used for hull-planing tests . . . Although conceived in 1918 for Fleet co-operation it was completed during the economies of the 1920s, purely to test the efficiency of the Linton Hope "flexible" hull as opposed to the existing "F" (Felixstowe) boats inspired by Porte'.

The 'Atalanta' was powered by four Rolls-Royce Condor 1A engines of about 650 h.p. each, which were mounted in two tandem pairs—two tractors and two pushers. Its wing span was 139 ft., its length 66 ft. and its maximum speed 100 m.p.h.

But the 'Atalanta' is no more. Mr. Donald Smith, of Ipswich, reported in 1970: 'The rarer 'Atalanta' was broken up and burnt when it deteriorated. I only learnt of this on reading the local paper, and went immediately to see if anything could be done before it was destroyed. Alas, I was too late and only charred bits of the burnt hull remained'.

Flying boats and seaplanes operating out of Great Yarmouth and Felixstowe were away for many hours at a time. A vital link in communication with the shore was the pigeon service. For this purpose and for intelligence work a series of lofts extended from Newcastle-upon-Tyne, Northumberland, to Hastings, Sussex, in World War I.

However, it was not until the closing period of the war that an air force branch of the pigeon service was established with the help of the navy and the army. Lofts were put in at all the important aerodromes in 1918, and airmen learnt to feel the confidence of having pigeons as companions. These all important message carriers, who carried out thousands of flights in World War I for the fighting services, were usually carried in baskets in aeroplanes.

When the Harwich loft of about 150 birds was moved to a site on the tennis court in front of the Felix Hotel, Felixstowe, in less than 10 days the pigeons homed correctly from 60 to 70 miles out to sea without making for Harwich.

Many are the stories of pigeons as resolute as the airmen they served. For instance, there was 'Wun Hi', the only survivor of two seaplanes, who although shot in the right eye safely delivered its last message. Another pigeon flew 22 miles in 22 minutes and saved the lives of two airmen. For example, six men aboard a Great Yarmouth-based H.12 flying boat, who were on the water disabled for three days, were saved by a cock pigeon after a flight of 100 miles. One of the first carrier pigeon messages released by the crippled seaplane—it was seaplane 8666—said: 'We have landed to pick up D.H. crew about 50 E by N of Yarmouth. Sea too rough to get off. Will you please send for us as soon as possible as boat is leaking. We are taxiing W by S'. The message was dated September 5, 1917.

In East Anglia, with so many flights being made by airmen from Great Yarmouth and Felixstowe over long distances in all weathers, care had to be taken about shooting carrier pigeons. Thus the *Eastern Daily Press* on October 21, 1918, stated: 'Numerous cases of shooting carrier pigeons have again been reported. The pigeons are sometimes the only means that a seaplane pilot has of communicating with the shore and obtaining assistance when in difficulties. If a pigeon in such cases fails to reach its loft it may mean the loss of some pilot's life. All sportsmen are therefore asked that, if they should in

Blackburn Iris III, S1263, at Felixstowe, was the first production model of her type. *Ministry of Defence*

Farman Seaplanes at Felixstowe. 1) Maurice Farman Shorthorn. 2) Maurice Farman Longhorn with No. 73 on its tail. 3) Henri Farman seaplane with No. 115 on its tail. *Mrs I Woollard and G. F. Cordy*

error bring down a carrier pigeon, to see that any message is immediately given to the nearest police station'.

As a patrol base Great Yarmouth was ideal, typical distances being Scheveningen 102 miles, Rotterdam 114 miles, Antwerp 138 miles, Dunkirk 107 miles, Ostend 95 miles and Le Havre 206 miles.

Long patrols were flown in World War I from Great Yarmouth and Felixstowe to Terschelling, Norderney and Borkum. A westerly wind caused the loss of many inexperienced pilots who, having chased an enemy airship or aircraft too far, could not make the return trip with the petrol supply they had left. Life-saving equipment was primitive and in winter the chances of being saved were almost nil.

Some idea of the suffering of North Sea airmen can be got from these references from *The Wing,* the monthly published by the Felixstowe air station, for September 15, 1917: 'It was with a deep sense of personal loss that many of us learned of the death of Flight Sub-Lieutenant A. B. Helbert—after a long fight against illness—induced, in a measure, it is thought, by exposure in the North Sea, in a seaplane last year.

'The latest report from Wing Commander John C. Porte, R.N., is that he is gradually recovering his strength in the milder air of the south coast.

'Arthur Crisp paid us a . . . visit the other day . . . . He told me that he was adrift in the North Sea for over three hours a short time ago . . .'.

The same issue said that Flight Lieutenant J. C. Railton was dead . . . .

It was not until June 4, 1918, that the greatest air battle took place between British flying boats and German seaplanes in World War I. It happened near the enemy coast, and the British force—it consisted of four F. 2as and an H.12 Large America from Great Yarmouth and Felixstowe—was led by Captain R. Leckie. The East Anglian aviators faced 14 fast enemy seaplanes of a crack unit, shot down six, and withdrew without much damage.

CHAPTER VII

Squadron Births — and Crashes

IT WAS at Thetford, incidentally, that No. 38 Squadron was formed on April 1, 1916, for home defence duties in the Wash area. It took action in all the Zeppelin raids from January, 1917, onwards until it moved to France in May, 1918, for night bombing duties. The squadron returned to England in 1919 and was disbanded. However, in September, 1935, it was reformed at Mildenhall, and later moved to Marham. No. 51 Squadron also operated from the Norwich area at night. The badge of 38 Squadron depicts a heron in flight and the motto reads 'Before the dawn'. The heron was chosen because in those days it was found in great abundance in East Anglia. A further reason was that herons rarely miss their mark, become active as twilight descends, and are formidable fighters when attacked. King George VI gave royal authority for the badge in February, 1937.

Quite apart from the flying done from Thetford during the all important army manoeuvres of 1912, which have already been described, it is clear that the authorities had the place earmarked as an aerodrome soon after the start of World War I in 1914. In fact, it was decided to adopt Thetford 'as the aerodrome and acceptance park for Norfolk'. Hangars were planned in large numbers, and hutments sited 'on Mr. Musker's estate'. The ascendancy of Mousehold aerodrome, following the rapid build up of aircraft production at Norwich, did, however, somewhat reduce the development of Thetford aerodrome.

Today there is little evidence at Thetford that this once powerful Saxon stronghold had an airfield. Mr. C. P. H. Wilson, of East Wretham, nr. Thetford, told me in 1966: 'In the Kaiser's war there was an aerodrome at Snarehill to the east of the A1088 Thetford-Euston road. All gone, save for a couple of squash courts, still in remarkably good condition'.

Marshal of the Royal Air Force, Lord Portal, commanded No. 7 Squadron at Bircham Newton in 1927, and Marshal of the Royal Air Force, Lord Tedder*, was commanding officer of No. 207 Squadron at the local station in 1920-1922.

Built in 1916, Bircham Newton was used for training on the formation of the R.A.F. in 1918, when No. 3 Fighter School was formed there. Towards the end of World War I No. 166 Squadron was formed as part of an independent bombing force to operate for the first time direct from England against targets in north west Germany. For this purpose the four-engined 'Super Handley', the Handley Page V/1500 was developed and although at the signing of the Armistice three of these giants were ready at Bircham Newton, no operations in fact took place. They had the range to reach Berlin. Then what amounted to the country's first 'V-bomber' squadrons, Nos. 166 and 274, were disbanded.

*Lord Tedder, G.C.B., who died in 1967 at the age of 76, was one of the outstanding figures of World War II. It was in the campaigns in North Africa that he made a name for himself in his partnership with Generals Auchinleck and Alexander and later with General Eisenhower.

What was the V/1500 like? Well, it had a span of 126 feet, a length of 64 feet, and stood 23 feet high. It had a useful load of 6½ tons, including a crew of six, thirty 250 lb. bombs, and several machine guns with ammunition. Fully loaded, it could make a flight of 650 miles; with a smaller load it could fly non-stop 1,200 miles. It had a total horse-power of 1,400 to 1,500, a cruising speed of 90 m.p.h., a maximum air speed of 100 m.p.h., and an endurance of 12 hours. The giant had a petrol capacity of 1,000 gallons.

Incidentally, the greatest secrecy was maintained during the building of the first V/1500, the components being made at Belfast by Harland and Wolff, the shipbuilders and marine engineers. The first successful flight took place in May, 1918, and had the war not ended in November of that year the R.A.F. would have got 255 V/1500s.

Bircham Newton's giant visitors had some remarkable features. Each of the four landing wheels was five feet in diameter, and the undercarriage was unusually strong. The bomber was thus able to take off from or land on makeshift aerodromes. In order to save weight, it amounted to 500 lb. for each engine, metal cowlings were not fitted.

No. 207 Squadron, which was stationed at Bircham Newton between the wars, was descended from No. 7 Squadron of the Royal Naval Air Service. For several years it was stationed at Bircham Newton, which it shared with No. 35 Squadron. Both were light bomber units, and for a time 207 Squadron flew Fairey Gordons. Having originally been 7 Squadron 207 was the first heavy night bomber unit to be formed in the British Air Services.

Feltwell, which lies to the north west of Brandon, had 'a fairly large aerodrome' in World War I. Some years after the war a 'flying field' with a beacon was maintained there. Then, in 1925, negotiations started for the purchase of land for a new aerodrome at Feltwell, and 10 years later the necessary land was acquired and building work started. The original plan for the aerodrome allowed for 11 Type C sheds but after five had been built World War II had started and the remainder were never erected. First squadron to use Feltwell was No. 37 which was reformed there on April 26, 1937, with Handley Page Harrow bombers. By August, 1939, the squadron had changed its Harrows for Vickers Wellington bombers.

East Anglia saw several squadrons formed at local airfields in World War I. For example, No. 64 Squadron (Motto 'Firm of Purpose') was formed in August, 1916, at Sedgeford not far from Docking in Norfolk. It remained there training fighter pilots until October, 1917, when equipped with D.H.5 fighters it flew to France* and quickly established a high reputation. During the big offensive from Cambrai in 1917, onwards, 64 Squadron was frequently called upon to assist the infantry by attacking enemy troops and guns. It had the distinction of having had only one commanding officer, the late Major B. E. Smythies, throughout its war service of about 2½ years. It returned to

*In *No Parachute: A Fighter Pilot In World War I*, Arthur Gould Lee noted: 'A new squadron, No. 64, with D.H.5s, commanded by Major Smythies, has just arrived from England, and is going into the accommodation next door to us, in the same orchard. At the moment, the officers have taken possession of our Mess, while their own is put into shape'. The author, who was a member of No. 46 Squadron equipped with fighters, made this reference in a letter he wrote on October 15, 1917.

England in February, 1919, and was disbanded in the following December. In March, 1936, the squadron was reformed in Egypt, and in the latter part of the 1930s was stationed at Martlesham Heath.

Living at Caister today is a former member of 64 Squadron, Mr. H. Carrington, who told me that Sedgeford airfield lay about three miles west of Docking and was situated on high open ground. Docking workhouse was used as a billet for practically the entire unit. The aerodrome had 'two or three hangars and some farm buildings were used as workshops and the like'. Early aircraft at Sedgeford included Farman and Avro biplanes. These gave place to F.E. 2bs. Then the squadron received D.H. 5s, departing for France about a year before the war ended. A new and larger aerodrome was then built at Bircham Newton.

'Major Smythies', explained Mr. Carrington, 'led the squadron right through to the end but later lost his life in a crash. While overseas he developed the idea of training fighter pilots with small scale models of enemy machines and using simulated guns

No. 64 Squadron formed at Sedgeford in the First World War. Some of the squadron with Major B. E. Smythies, the C.O., and Adjutant, Lieutenant R. Turner. *H. Carrington*

N.C.Os off duty at Sedgeford in 1916. *H. Carrington*

and machines. I often had to go out to crashed enemy machines and get full details and then have an exact scale replica made in our workshop. We had quite a collection at the end of the war. I only managed to get one home—a Fokker biplane model— but this disappeared in one of my moves. The only souvenir I have of Sedgeford is a clock mounted in a shaped wooden propeller boss from a crashed machine. My brother in law at Hunstanton has a large four bladed propeller hanging in his garage premises.

'The nearest place for amusement in those days was Hunstanton, and there was a nightly trek to this spot if you were lucky enough to get some form of transport. I often went there from Sedgeford on an old belt-driven Triumph motor cycle or a push bike. The town sported a small cinema called the Mikado, later burnt down, which was also used by a concert party in the summer. The electric power for lights was provided by a gas engine at the back and, strangely enough, this engine used to conk out when the boys were around. . . . I might mention that I am married to the girl who used to play the musical accompaniment at the pictures. Incidentally, my sister claims that I was the first Norwich man to fly in an aeroplane. My first flight was in, I believe, late 1913 or early 1914 when I joined the Royal Flying Corps'.

Harleston, not far from the airship station at Pulham, was the birthplace of Captain Gordon P. Olley who was one of the first pilots to fly one million miles. Born there in 1893, Captain Olley, who flew with Imperial Airways, demonstrated, for example, that the aeroplane had its uses as a means of transport for big-game hunters. This meant that this charter pilot, who flew a distance of about 30,000 miles to many parts of Africa, had to be resourceful in picking up his passengers when the hunting was over. For protection at night against wild animals, a hedge of thorny bushes had to be built round Captain Olley's machine. Apparently the hedge 'kept off lions and hyenas, which are said to gnaw the rubber tyres of landing wheels if they have the opportunity'.

I do not suppose any one has managed to calculate with any accuracy just how many aircraft have crashed in East Anglia since flying started. But pieces from time to time turn up in private hands and in this way plots are possible. Mr. A. Mattinson, of Saxmundham, let me have in 1968 a piece of one of the struts of an aircraft which, another source stated, came down at Horsey on the Norfolk coast on September 22, 1914, 'on Crinkle Hill road, with its nose in a field belonging to Mrs. Andrews, of Kerrison Farm, and its tail in a field farmed by Mr. English, of Street Farm. We were told the pilot was a Mr. Cadbury'. Mr. Mattinson remembered that the plane's wheels were taken off by the low banks as it crossed the lane, that it had two wheels side by side on each leg, and that the pilot said to the observer 'something about revs'. He also believed that the aircraft had an elevator in front, that it was a biplane, and that it was a pusher type.

Crash of a D.H.1 at Mr Walter Carter's Rose Farm, Acle, Norfolk, during the First World War.

C. F. Morris

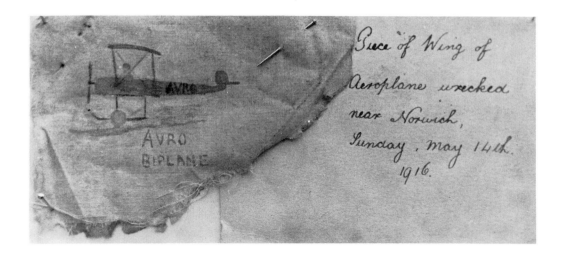

Fabric from an Avro 504 biplane which crashed at Hellesdon, near Norwich on May 14, 1916.   *Author*

Take the case of Flight Lieutenant C. E. Wood, flying a B.E.2C from Bacton on the night of January 31, 1916. Having failed to find reported Zeppelins, he prepared to return to base, but just then his engine stopped. In total darkness, not knowing exactly where he was, he glided down and passed down an avenue of trees—in the right direction—so that they clipped off his wings! This happened at Spixworth, three miles from Norwich, and the pilot landed unhurt in the wingless fuselage.

Mr. Robert Malster, of Ipswich, filled in another gap in the 1960s when he sent me a piece of fabric from an Avro biplane which had been passed to him through his father. Roughly painted on the souvenir is a water colour of an Avro 504 biplane, and with it a card inscribed: 'Piece of wing of aeroplane wrecked near Norwich, Sunday, May 14th, 1916'. The actual scene was 'out along the Aylsham road'.

The crash, by all accounts, was somewhat violent. For the *East Anglian Daily Times* for May 15, 1916, noted: 'A shocking flying accident occurred on the outskirts of Norwich on Sunday afternoon, resulting in the death of two men well known in the aviation world—Mr. F. G. Sumner, Chief Inspector in the Aeronautical Inspection Department attached to the War Office, and Lieutenant O. G. Hake of the R.F.C. They were testing a machine at the time ... and were manoeuvring in the neighbourhood of Hellesdon ... when one of the wings collided with a fir tree in the grounds of Major Berners, at Hellesdon House. The wing was torn off, and the machine, after ploughing its way through a belt of small trees, struck an outbuilding adjacent to Hellesdon Mills and fell to the ground. ...'. Lieutenant Hake, who knew Major Berners, was piloting the Avro.

Aeroplane crashes and forced landings, certainly in the early days, led to adults as well as children making for the spot despite work and school. Thus, when a Sopwith Pup made a forced landing off the B1145 road in World War I, the following note was put in the log at Colby School: 'March 8, 1918—The attendance has been much lowered this week by the children going to North Walsham to see an aeroplane'.

The earliest plane crash which I can remember, I was eight or nine at the time, occurred near the Sir John Leman School, Beccles, on the afternoon of May 4, 1937. While flying in company with two other machines, a Hawker Hind biplane light bomber belonging to No. 139 (Jamaica) Squadron, R.A.F. Wyton, Huntingdonshire, lost touch in poor visibility. At 4.30 p.m. the pilot, Sergeant James Parkinson, wishing to check his bearings, landed in a meadow on the Roos Hall Estate, just off the Beccles-Ringsfield Road, the scene of joy flights in the early 1930s. However, in braking hard, the Hind turned over and its wooden propeller was smashed. But the pilot and his companion, Aircraftman Frank McAdoo, aged 18, escaped serious injury although they had to be helped out of their aircraft through the escape panels in the fuselage.

Remains of D.H.5 A9393 crashed by a Canadian pilot of 64 Squadron in 1917.   *H. Carrington*

1) Frank Neale's Avro 504K G-EAEB after a forced landing on Lakenham cricket ground, Norwich in the early 1920s. 2) Mr H. Sykes' Avro 504K G-EACA badly smashed after a crash at Three Fields, Earlham in the early 1920s.

George Swain

The Hind, which was photographed by my brother who with other boys reached the scene soon after the crash, was K5370 and was one of 528 built, the first having flown in 1934 and entering service in 1936.

Another crash which I can remember happened later that year. It involved an aircraft from Martlesham Heath—I have a piece of silver painted fabric from it marked 'Plane "K"—November 22, 1937'—and it came down in a field belonging to Mr. S. Ingate about 150 yards from the Halesworth-Walpole road just outside the Halesworth boundary. The aircraft, before crashing, 'travelled very low for some distance, one woman declaring that it just missed her farmhouse'. It then turned over, trapping the passenger, Aircraftman Robert E. Smith, but the pilot, Sergeant Herber, got out. Several local farmers ran to the scene, lifted up the machine, and released the man whose head appeared to be buried in the ground—in fact, a penknife had to be used to scrape earth out of the airman's nostrils. A farm gate was improvised as a stretcher and the injured man was carried to the roadway, reaching Halesworth Hospital in a bacon lorry.

Hawker Hind K5370 of 139 (Jamaica) Squadron, Wyton, Huntingdonshire which overturned on May 4, 1937 while making a forced landing near Beccles, Suffolk.

D. V. Elliott

CHAPTER VIII

Zeppelins and other Raiders

COMPARED with the performance of the various air forces in the last war the tonnage of bombs dropped in World War I was puny. Between 1914 and 1918 less than 9,000 German bombs of a total weight of about 280 tons were dropped on British soil in the course of 51 airship and 52 aeroplane attacks. German airships crossed the east and south coasts on 202 occasions. British fighters went up after airships on 625 occasions. Altogether, before the Germans switched to using the Gotha G IV twin-engined bomber, they lost 10 airships—eight to fighters and two to anti-aircraft guns. Three of the airships—the L.21, L.48 and L.70—fell within the area covered by this book. Norfolk and Suffolk probably heard more Zeppelins than any other part of the country, and when an official map was considered for publication after the war, showing their paths, it was too crowded to make sense.

When was the first Zeppelin attack on this country? Well, there was no enemy airship activity over any part of Great Britain in 1914, although a few reconnaissances by naval airships were carried out over the North Sea during December of that year. But an enemy aircraft dropped a single bomb at Dover—the first to fall on British soil—on December 24.

At a meeting of the Standing Joint Committee of East Suffolk on February 25, 1919, a detailed report was presented on local police observation work in connection with raids by hostile airships and aircraft. East Suffolk, for example, had 39 raids—28 by Zeppelins, nine by aeroplanes and two by bombardment from the sea.* Bombs and shells numbered 498 H.Es, 235 incendiaries and 43 magnesium flares. Aerial bombs varied in weight between 660 lb. and 26 lb., while enemy ships up to cruiser size fired 11-inch, 6-inch and 4½-inch shells at towns along the Suffolk coast.

The average duration of a raid was about five hours. Moonless nights, with a high barometer and little or no wind, were those generally chosen by the enemy for Zeppelin attacks. For the first year or two the Zeppelins, when caught in searchlights, resembled silver cigars, but by June, 1917, when the L.48 was shot down over Suffolk, Zeppelins were painted black save for their top areas. Total raid damage in East Suffolk was about £45,000.

The Zeppelin campaign, which was the start of a new form of aerial warfare, was launched on the night of January 19/20, 1915, when the L.3, L.4 and L.6 left Nordholz and Fuhlsbuttel. The L.6 had engine trouble and turned back, but the L.3 ((Kapitanleutnant Fritz) and the L.4 (Kapitanleutnant Graf von Platen) approached the Norfolk coast over the Haisbro' lightship. Then they ran into rain, snow squalls and fog banks. The L.3 entered at Ingham, and at about 8.30 p.m. flew over Great Yarmouth,

---

*In the bombardment of Lowestoft from the sea on April 25, 1916—a Zeppelin came over Suffolk before the shelling—seven out of about 60 11-inch shells failed to explode, others went clean over Lowestoft, and I have heard it said that some went into Haddiscoe marshes. Four people were killed and 21 injured. Damage to property amounted to nearly £25,000. Then, on January 25, 1917, two enemy destroyers fired 68 6-inch and 4½-inch shells in the direction of Southwold. Only four shells fell on Southwold, the rest whistled over to Uggeshall over four miles away from the assumed position of the enemy ships.

where seven of the nine bombs it dropped killed two people and injured three. The L.4 took a path over north east Norfolk, dropped odd bombs at various coastal places until King's Lynn was reached. It was thought that the commander mistook the area for the mouth of the Humber and unloaded seven of his nine H.E. bombs and the last of his incendiary bombs on King's Lynn. Two people were killed and 13 were injured.

During this attack on Great Yarmouth bombs fell near the Drill Hall, York Road, and near St. Peter's Church. These bombs killed an old cobbler, Mr. Samuel Smith, and a Miss Martha Taylor. There is a story that a local surgeon, who extracted a minute fragment of bomb from the leg of a casualty, had it mounted in a tie pin.

Why did the Zeppelins spend so much time over East Anglia—and particularly Stowmarket? Well, firms handling government work were located at such places as Bury St. Edmunds, Norwich, Lowestoft, Thetford, Great Yarmouth, King's Lynn, Ipswich, Beccles, Leiston and Dereham. The New Explosive Co. at Stowmarket must have been of added appeal because of the possibility of making a really big explosion with a bomb in the right place. But although Zeppelins hovered about the town they never scored any direct hits on the factory.

One other target of interest to the Zeppelins in Norfolk was the royal home at Sandringham. However, it has been said that Queen Alexandra, who was in residence

110lb. Zeppelin bomb (left) dropped at East Dereham on September 9, 1915. Incendiary bomb (right) dropped at Henham, near Southwold by L5 or L13. *Mrs S. M. Griffith and F. Jenkins*

there for much of the war, was practically unable to accept the idea that they had an interest in the house and its residents. Searchlights and guns round the royal estate were used with great care so as not to draw attention to the precise position of the house. Mostly, it appears, the Zeppelin crews were misled and bombed widely.

The Haisbro' lightship, as already indicated, was a recognised check point for Zeppelins coming in and going out. While it gave the Zeppelins help it disciplined them to follow a pattern which our ground and air defences exploited to the full. In fact, it soon became clear that the stretch of coast opposite the lightship, the seven miles between Trimingham and Happisburgh, was ideal for engaging the Zeppelins, with Bacton the ideal spot for guns and fighters.

As a quick answer to the Zeppelin menace machine guns with high angle mountings were installed on fast vehicles fitted with searchlights. The eastern mobile section, which was responsible for the whole of East Anglia, had its headquarters at Newmarket from early 1915 under the command of Major W. G. Lucas, R.N.A.S. However, the Admiralty ceased to have control of land attacks on hostile airships and aircraft in early 1916, after which the Field Marshal Commanding-in-Chief, Homes Forces, London, took over.

The Royal Naval Mobile Anti-Aircraft Brigade, which assembled in the London area, went by way of the Great North Road, then through Newmarket and Thetford, on to Norwich, and finally to North Walsham from which point the guns were set up over a 20 mile front. The mobile brigade consisted of 12 self-propelled guns, three mobile searchlights, and 20 other vehicles, including ammunition waggons and motor cycles. The distribution of guns along the famous stretch of coast for a typical night was: two 75 mm guns north of Bacton, one 3 pounder south of Mundesley, one 3 pounder at Watch House Gap, one searchlight north of Mundesley, and one searchlight at Walcott Gap.

Three airships, including the L.5 under Kapitanleutnant Bocker, who in 1916 bombed Sudbury, flew against this country on the night of April 15/16, 1915. The L.5 dropped bombs at Henham Hall, Southwold and Lowestoft, the airship while in the Southwold area being fired on by the 6th Battalion Sussex Cyclists quartered at Easton Bavents. Flight Commander de C. W. P. Ireland went up in a seaplane from Great Yarmouth but saw nothing of Bocker.

On the 'beautiful moonlight night' of April 29/30, 1915, the first raid by army airship was carried out. The airship came in over Felixstowe at 11.55 p.m. and, going inland, dropped 10 H.E. and 66 incendiary bombs at Bury St. Edmunds.

Reference has already been made to the distribution of munition factories in Eastern England. So it happened on March 31/April 1, 1916, that five naval airships steered for England with such factories in mind. Kapitanleutnant Heinrich Mathy, in the L. 13, came in at Saxmundham, followed the 8.15 p.m. train from Ipswich, and heading for

Stowmarket dropped bombs there. When over Stowmarket the L.13, having dropped 12 bombs close to the explosives factory, was hit by a tracer shell. Some disturbance must have been caused aboard the raider because the following message written by Mathy himself and intended to be sent by wireless was picked up near the factory next morning: 'High Sea Chief—have thrown battery at Stowmarket with success—Been hit, am turning back—landing Hage 4 a.m.—L. 13'.

The police, as usual, were on the alert and told the defences the possible subsequent course of the L. 13 so that the R.N.A.S. at Lowestoft were able to send out armed vehicles. They drove out of Lowestoft, with headlights on, and as anticipated caught the Zeppelin's attention at Wangford. Near the village the L.13 dropped 18 H.E. bombs and 25 incendiary bombs, the last ones falling at Frostenden and Covehithe. She had previously dropped three petrol tanks at Earl Stonham and Stonham Parva.

Meanwhile, what did some of the other Zeppelins get up to? L. 16 (Oberleutnant Peterson) came in over Winterton soon after 10 o'clock, reaching Bury St. Edmunds close on midnight. Here her commander dropped bombs, turned, and went out over Lowestoft. The L. 14 (Kapitanleutnant Bocker) dropped bombs at several places, including Sudbury, and retired at Saxmundham. Kapitanleutnant Breithaupt's L.15, coming in over Dunwich at 7.45 p.m., was engaged over Essex and finally broke her back, falling from 2,000 feet into the sea at the Knock Deep off Foulness at 11 o'clock. Two trawlers saved her crew but one man was drowned. Afterwards it was said that one of the crew, an officer, disclosed to the authorities that he had a sister living in

German Zeppelin L 71 arriving at Pulham July 1, 1920.   *George Swain*

the Eastern Counties. Curiously, on that night, the telephonic and telegraphic com-
munications to the naval air stations at Cranwell, Lincolnshire, Great Yarmouth
and Felixstowe were out of action following gale damage. What was even more sus-
picious, all but one of the airships came in in the vicinity of these air stations.

When I made inquiries in 1955 about a photograph I had been given of bombed
property in Sudbury in World War I, Mr. S. W. Slaughter, of London, W.C.2., replied:
'The attack was carried out by the L.14 under the command of Kapitanleutnant Bocker
... I have a rough idea of what happened because my grandparents were living in
Sudbury at the time and I was visiting the town. I seem to remember that one of the
bombs fell on a house in Waldingfield Road—the house next door to The Horse and
Groom—and took off the top storeys of a row of houses opposite'.

On the night of July 28/29, 1916, the L.31 was one of six Zeppelins which were
airborne. She came in over Hopton at 1.18 a.m., was over Beccles nine minutes later,
was near Kessingland at 1.50 a.m., and was off Lowestoft at 2 o'clock. At the time there
was heavy ground mist along the Waveney Valley which, it was thought, accounted
for the L.31's dissolute course.

When Zeppelins were reported in the vicinity of Wells on the night of July 30,
1916, aeroplanes went up from Holt, Bacton, Great Yarmouth and Covehithe. However,
no raid followed. Then, at 5.15 a.m. next day, a B.E.2C from Covehithe, flown by
Flight Sub-Lieutenant J. C. Northrop, met and engaged an enemy airship 30 miles
out to sea. The Zeppelin escaped because the ammunition tray on the Lewis gun came
away and struck him in the face.

A few days later—on the night of August 2/3—the L.21 was heard at Bungay at
12.25 a.m. and seen at Brampton an hour later.

Twelve airships set out against England on the night of August 24/25, 1916,
but only four crossed the coast. One came in at Aldeburgh and dropped bombs between
Woodbridge and Ipswich at about midnight. At one point the airship could not be
found, owing to her keeping above the clouds. A searchlight was kept searching along
a break towards Ipswich, so that, if the airship crossed the clear patch, she would be
picked up. After repeatedly manoeuvring to cross the break the airship, fearing she
was trapped, made straight for the searchlight and tried to put it out of action with
bombs. The airship, however, failed to knock out the searchlight, but in the confusion
managed to get away.

On the night of September 2/3, 1916, the greatest and most numerous airship
fleet the world ever saw set course for England. In all 16 Zeppelins started—12 naval
and 4 army—and all but two, one naval and one army, crossed the coast. The naval
airships were the L.11, L.13, L.14, L.16, L.17, L.21, L.22, L.23, L.24, L.30, L.32 and
S.L. 8. The L.17, however, turned back off the Norfolk coast. Of the army airships
only one was definitely identified—the S.L.11. The following naval airships were spotted

On the night of September 2/3, 1916, the greatest airship fleet ever assembled concentrated over East Anglia. Track of these airships is here shown.   *H.M.S.O.*

L 70 which was attacked off the Norfolk coast on the night of August 5/6, 1918 and fell in flames off Wells. Major Egbert Cadbury (shown above) and on the right his observer/gunner Captain R. Leckie, in a D.H.4 from Great Yarmouth, this type is shown below, shot the L 70 down.

Imperial War Museum, J. Peters and Ministry of Defence

at Lowestoft, the L.30 and L.32, at Cromer, the L.24, and at Great Yarmouth, the L.11. An army airship followed the Great Eastern railway past Chelmsford, Colchester, and Ipswich where it turned over Saxmundham and went out to sea. Another army airship, which had come in over Frinton, lowered an observation car near Mistley, east of Manningtree, but the cable broke and the car, it contained a mattress and various instruments, and 5,000 feet of wire fell at Mistley. The airship carried on to Great Yarmouth, shedding the winch of the lost car and more cable at Wixoe, near Clare.

The usual efforts were made by the East Anglian defenders to tackle the airships. Flight Lieutenant E. Cadbury, flying from Great Yarmouth, saw a hostile airship held by the Lowestoft searchlights but lost her in the clouds. Flight Sub-Lieutenant S. Kemball, who had taken off from Covehithe, went up but saw nothing. Flight Sub-Lieutenant E. L. Pulling made no less than three ascents from Bacton in a B.E. 2C in search of airships between midnight and 4.15 a.m. next day. So well did the defending fighters frighten the enemy fleet that in dropping 463 H.E. and incendiary bombs, weighing a total of 16 tons, they killed only four people and injured 12.

A B.E. 2C biplane, flown by Flight Sub-Lieutenant E.L. Pulling, went up from Bacton on the night of November 27/28, 1916, and engaged the L.21, commanded by Kapitanleutnant Frankenburg, which had been over this country for nearly nine hours. Holt sent fighters, too, and Flight Lieutenant E. Cadbury and Flight Sub-Lieutenant G. W. R. Fane rose as well from Burgh Castle. It was reported that, as the L.21 fell in flames, stern foremost, some of her gunners continued to fire. Only an oil mark on the sea marked her resting place 10 miles off between Lowestoft and Southwold. As the airship fell, Fane, whose face, flying helmet and aircraft were scorched by the fierce heat, saw a gunner in the top cockpit leave his position and run straight over the nose of the airship—without a parachute.

Flying boats from Great Yarmouth and Felixstowe scored two victories against Zeppelins. On May 14, 1917, the L.22 was shot down in flames off Terschelling by a Large America H.12 from Great Yarmouth. The crew of the flying boat consisted of Flight Lieutenant C. J. Galpin, Flight Sub-Lieutenant R. Leckie, who took part in the destruction of the L.70 in 1918, Chief Petty Officer V. Whatling, and Air Mechanic J. R. Laycock. When about 80 miles out from Great Yarmouth the flying boat broke off wireless contact in order to avoid detection. The L.22 which fell into the sea, left a mass of black ash from which sprang up and stood a column of brown smoke about 1,500 feet.

Then, on June 14, 1917, a Large America H.12 from Felixstowe, piloted by Flight Sub-Lieutenant B. D. Hobbs and Flight Sub-Lieutenant R. F. L. Dickey, claimed the L.43 off Vlieland. Other crew members were Air Mechanic H. M. Davis and Air Mechanic A. W. Goody. As the L.43 fell in flames three men were seen to fall or jump out without parachutes.

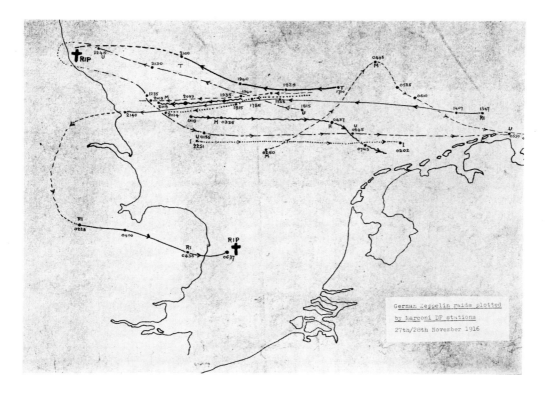

The L 21 and the L 34 were plotted on the night of November 27/28 1916 by Marconi DF stations until they were shot down off Hartlepool, Co. Durham and Lowestoft.　　　　　*The Marconi Co. Ltd.*

The only Zeppelin to fall on East Anglian soil in the World War I was the L.48 on the night of June 16/17, 1917, having only been commissioned at Friedrichshafen a month earlier. The giant, which was over 600 feet long, fell in flames at Theberton, near Leiston. The raid which cost the Germans the L.48 involved four naval airships of which two, probably because of lack of cloud cover, turned back without crossing the coast. She was under the command of Kapitanleutnant Franz Eichler and she carried a most important officer—Korvettenkapitan Victor Schutze, Commodore of the North Sea Airship Division.

The L.48 came in by way of Orfordness at about 2 o'clock in the morning, rounded Wickham Market, and then went south past Woodbridge. She dropped bombs in the vicinity of Martlesham Heath with, however, little effect. Anti-aircraft guns, it is thought, first damaged her, and as she came over Theberton people on the ground reported hearing the sound of tapping as the crew tried frantically to carry out temporary repairs.

At least three fighters are said to have engaged the L.48 during the time she was over this country. The F.E. 2b, which was reported to have been made at Ipswich, had as its pilot Second Lieutenant F. D. Holder with Sergeant S. Ashby as his gunner. Captain R. H. M. S. Saundby* was in a D.H. 2 single seater. Yet Lieutenant L. P. Watkins of No. 37 Squadron, Goldhanger, Essex, who first engaged the airship at nearly 14,000 feet, is generally understood to have been the victor. Possibly, in view of the L.48's size, all the pilots attacked at different stages without seeing their comrades' individual attacks. All, furthermore, thought that their bullets were responsible for the airship's destruction. Certainly at the time Captain Saundby and Lieutenant Holder were both stationed at the experimental station at Orfordness. A few weeks later Lieutenant Holder had a narrow escape when his aircraft crashed at East Bridge, near Theberton. Ashby, the gunner in Holder's aircraft in the fight with the L.48, was killed shortly afterwards in a crash at Martlesham Heath. In 1950, when I made

This photograph of the three German naval airships, L 10, L 12 and L 13, was taken from the L 11 as they set out on a raid on England. *Imperial War Museum*

*Retired as Air Marshal Sir Robert Saundby, K.C.B., K.B.E., M.C., D.F.C., A.F.C.

inquiries at Theberton, there was a feeling locally that one of the pilots concerned may have taken off without permission. The story was that one of the pilots clad in pyjamas and canvas shoes landed his machine on the marshes some distance away and made his way on foot to the crashed airship.

As the background to the shooting down of the L.48 was conflicting, even at official level, I asked Air Marshal Sir Robert Saundby, of Burghclere, near Newbury, who was the captain concerned, if he could put the story straight. He told me in 1970: 'On the night of June 16/17, 1917, two aircraft belonging to my Flight at Orfordness took off when a Zeppelin raid was reported. It was part of my duty to send off two aircraft, a B.E.2E and an F.E.2b, in order to back up the regular Home Defence squadrons. The F.E. was piloted by Lieutenant Holder.

'The whole thing was rather a farce, as the Zeppelins, by that time, had taken to flying at 15,000 ft., and the ceiling of these two types of aircraft was about 12,000/ 13,000 ft. Seeing the airship overhead at a great height, and knowing that my two aircraft could not reach it, I ordered out a D.H.2 that I had in my Flight for various tests, and decided to take off and see if I could reach it. I had never flown at night myself, and the aircraft had no cockpit or navigation lights, but I knew that I could stay in the air till dawn.

'At 14,500 ft. I was close under the airship, and I fired off eight double drums of incendiary ammunition and near the end of my last drum, while I was still firing at the Zeppelin, it burst into flames. I followed it down, and saw it hit the ground near Leiston. I did not see any other aircraft in the vicinity of the airship, but Lieutenant Watkins, in a B.E. 12, claimed to have attacked the Zeppelin from above. This may well have been so, though I saw nothing of it, and saw no incendiary bullets other than my own.

'An inquiry was carried out by General W. S. (later Sir Sefton) Brancker who decided that the D.H. 2 from Orfordness had shot down the Zeppelin. The Home Defence Command raised a strong objection to this, on the ground, presumably that we at Orfordness were merely amateurs and that they were the professionals, and it was eventually decided to allow their claim. That is how 37 Squadron and Orfordness came to share the credit'.

What actually happened when the L.48 started to fall near Leiston? Her death plunge took from three to five minutes. As she descended, heading for a field near Holly Tree Farm, Theberton, she put out a trail of smoke a mile long and a glow enveloped the huge airship. She struck the ground stern first at an angle of about 60 degrees so that all in her rear gondola, which carried Korvettenkapitan Schutze, lost their lives. The front gondola, was badly damaged but one of the crew, Oberleutnant Mieth, the observation officer, survived though terribly injured. Two other men, who were in the side gondolas, survived thanks to the efforts of P.C. Kiddle, one severely injured and the other apparently unhurt. The airship crew believed they were near Harwich, over the sea, and made preparations for 'ditching'. Schutze

The L 48, a brand new Zeppelin which was shot down in flames at Theberton after midnight on June 17, 1917—she was over 600 feet long. Note the ring of soldiers guarding the wreckage.

Imperial War Museum and Mrs Anne Hammond

was incinerated, Eichler and four others were killed when they jumped without parachutes.

When I visited Theberton in 1950 there were 16 members of the L.48's crew buried in the local churchyard. In 1967, when the German cemetery for her war dead of two wars was dedicated at Cannock Chase, Staffordshire, it was reported that Kapitan-leutnant Eichler and his crew had been reinterred there with three other Zeppelin crews. The simple stone memorial tablets I saw at Theberton over 20 years ago were sent from Germany. They came by sea to Southampton, by train to Leiston, by horse and tumbrill to Theberton. The site of the L.48's plunge is remembered today as Zeppelin Field.

Mr. Cecil H. Lay, of Aldringham, said in 1951 that he was one of the first on the spot when the L.48 fell. Apparently a 'golden Iron Cross', presumably a medal worn by one of the senior officers, was found among the wreckage. Mr. Lay recalled that the morning of June 17 'was a superb one and . . . the sky was cloudless and beautiful as only an early morning June sky can be'.

Mrs. Daphne Taylor, of Kettleburgh, said that on the Sunday following the crash 'the corn was ruthlessly trampled down by people as they took short cuts to the scene from all directions'. When an appeal was made for scrap in 1939-1945 Mrs. Taylor 'fetched down from the attic about 4 feet of girder from the Zeppelin'. A similar piece about the same time was turned out at Framlingham. So it looks as if the L.48, as it lay broken at Theberton, was the source of many souvenirs.

Mr. Archibald C. Brown, of Bungay, commenting in 1952 on my survey of the Theberton crash site, said: 'Incidentally, when the L.48 was shot down at Theberton . . . I was serving with the R.F.C. and was stationed at Weybridge . . . When I came home a few weeks later my father told me that he had seen the airship coming down in flames—from here in Bungay. At daybreak, he, with others, started off on cycles think-ing they would come across the wreck before they got to Halesworth. However, they had to pedal on to Theberton before they reached it'.

Still another eyewitness of the period, Mrs. G. Goddard, of Ipswich, who was 10 at the time of the Zeppelin crash at Theberton, said she remembered that their garden at Blythburgh 'was littered with the Zeppelin's burnt fuselage'. Thus, it seems, pieces of the airship fell over a wide area as, it will be remembered, the L.48 took some minutes to reach the ground. Mrs. Goddard added that her most vivid recollection of the whole affair was 'seeing the only survivor . . . being marched to Darsham station under escort'.

Seaplanes from Great Yarmouth made attacks on enemy ports and shipping. Sometimes the Germans returned this attention by flying against our own ports. So on February 20, 1916, two enemy seaplanes in daylight, it was Sunday morning at church time, dropped 19 bombs in the Lowestoft area. Six fighters from Great Yar-mouth went up in pursuit, including Flight Lieutenant E. Cadbury, who wrote: 'It

Top left is a drawing by Leonard Squirrell of the F.E.2b B401 said at the time to have shot down L.48. Top right Lieutenant Frank Holder, who took part in the engagement of L 48, sailing with Captain W. W. Hammond on the River Alde. Centre the remains of the L 48.

University of Reading, Ransomes Collection and Mrs Anne Hammond

was simply terribly cold—I had no time to get ready and had not got any gloves; I have never been so cold before'.

Six days later, on February 26, two hostile aeroplanes made an abortive attack on H.M.S. *Gordoba* near the Sunk lightship. Next day two German aviators, who had spent a rough night at sea, were landed at Lowestoft by the tug *New Boy*. They had set out from Ostend the previous morning with the *Gordoba* assailants, but their seaplane developed engine trouble and they were forced down.

Felixstowe, which was a vital East Coast air station, received attention from German Gotha G IV twin-engined bombers on July 4, 1917. The 16 strong enemy formation crossed the Suffolk coast at Shingle Street at 7 o'clock in the morning although they were first encountered off the coast by Captain J. Palethorpe who was carrying out an endurance test on a D.H.4 from Martlesham Heath. He at once attacked the centre machine and, in fact, succeeded in making the formation alter course temporarily. His observer, First Air Mechanic J. O. Jessop, being shot through the heart, forced Palethorpe to return to the Suffolk coast. The Gothas, on reaching Felixstowe, dropped 42 bombs which killed 17 men and injured another 30 at the air station. A seaplane was destroyed. Twenty-one pedigree sheep were killed and 29 injured by some of the bombs which fell on Trimley marshes.

Then came the famous Gotha daylight raid on London on July 7, 1917—the raid which set the country talking and which led to a searching inquiry into the dual control of the air defences by the Army and the Navy. The Gotha formation, the force at the start was 22 strong, was sighted well out to sea. They crossed the coast at Coate Outfall, near the mouth of the River Crouch, Essex, and in no time 78 R.F.C. and R.N.A.S. were struggling to intercept. Once again Captain Palethorpe, operating from Martlesham Heath in a D.H.4, engaged the Gothas, his gunner being Air Mechanic F. James. This time a stray bullet hit Palethorpe in the hip. In 1955, while visiting Mr. Henry J. Reynolds, artist of the old school, at Halstead, Essex, I was given an original water colour by the artist showing the Gotha formation bombing near St. Paul's Cathedral on that July day.

CHAPTER IX

Airships at Pulham

THE AIRSHIP was born in 1852 as the result of the work of a Frenchman, Henri Giffard, aeronaut, who proved that a balloon's movements in the air could be directed. His small non-rigid craft was powered by a 3 h.p. steam engine. which drove two wing propellers 10 ft. in diameter. The machine—it was just over 144 ft. long—had the appearance somewhat reminiscent of a circus trapeze. This description was applied because 19 ft. below the gasbag a rod 65 ft. long was suspended on which, at a distance of over 11 ft., hung the car.

France and Germany had for some years been developing the airship before the British government entered the field in 1907. Colonel J. E. Capper, R.E., then head of the Balloon Factory, Aldershot, built the first government airship—the 'Nulli Secundus'. On her trials in September, 1907, she attained a speed of 16 m.p.h. In May, 1909, the 'Baby' appeared but was soon rebuilt with a volume of 33,000 cubic ft. In 1910, with a 30 h.p. Green engine, she was renamed 'Beta'. The Army developed successive non-rigid airships, the 'Beta' being followed by 'Gamma I'.

In September, 1912, 'Beta' and 'Gamma' visited Cambridge in connection with the army manoeuvres. Mr. H. Lister, of Cambridge, recalled in 1970: 'These two airships landed on Midsummer Common, Cambridge, about 6 o'clock one morning. There were so many people crowded round that the captains of the airships gave orders for the ships to rise and go into the grounds of Jesus College. Those were the first airships I saw'. 'Beta', incidentally, had the distinction of being the first airship to be inspected by King George V and Queen Mary.

Here it is interesting to recall that *Flight* for September 28, 1912, in reporting the month's progress in aviation, said that 'Gamma', while making a flight from Cambridge to Salisbury Plain a few days before, had collided with a haystack at Devizes, Wiltshire. The journal also noted that, as 'Gamma' left Cambridge, she dropped 'bombs' on the town. 'Beta', while operating with the troops near Cambridge, one night in order to locate camps, dropped 'fireballs into each bivouac or camp she visited'. 'Gamma' carried wireless and was thus able to communicate with the ground. The army manoeuvres in which 'Beta' and 'Gamma' took part are described in chapter 2.

In 1915 30 coastal 'blimps' with an 11 hour endurance were ordered for the new stations, mostly in coastal areas, which were being built. They were needed in the North Sea for use against German submarines.

What was the origin of Pulham airship station? It grew up in World War I around Home Farm and the adjoining Lincoln's Farm, Pulham St. Mary, where existing buildings were used as workshops. The station was opened in February, 1916, but did not receive its first coastal 'blimp', they were called 'Pulham Pigs' on account of their shape, until August 31, 1916, followed by more coastals in November and December.

Originally the station had two large hangars but one was removed to Cardington airship station, Bedfordshire, in the late 1920s at a cost of £100,000. There was even a railway to the Norfolk station from Pulham Market, and ex-Squadron Leader Herbert J. Brown, of London, S.E.20, told me in 1966, when he was 84, that he remembered the occasion when a freight train eight to ten wagons 'slowly turned on its side when the ballast subsided'.

Writing in the first number of the *Pulham Patrol,* a threepenny magazine, which appeared in September, 1917, the Mayor of Norwich (Ald. G. M. Chamberlin), whose letter was dated July 28, said: 'I am glad to say that we very often have visits paid us by Pulham airmen, and a very smart lot they are . . .'.

Pulham took the most experienced airship men. One respected member was Chief Petty Officer Edwards who was one of several pioneers of the Airship Section of the original R.F.C., the Naval Wing of which was the predecessor or parent of the R.N.A.S. Petty Officer Edwards, who was chief of the landing party at Pulham, enlisted in the Royal Marines in 1906, his first connection with airship work being in 1910 on naval

A typical "Pulham Pig" of the early years over its landing ground.   *W. C. H. Hubbard*

The Coastal C 1 was first towed by the light cruiser *Carysfort* in Harwich in May, 1916 to give her greater
range.   *Suffolk Photo Survey*

airship No. 1. In fact, he worked on all the early airships, including 'Beta' and 'Gamma'.

Submarine activity in the North Sea necessitated the accommodation of small
non-rigid airships near the sea coast. By August, 1918, there were 11 mooring sites in
commission, including Pulham. More sites were required, and sites with thick trees
and adjacent open ground could not always be found where desired. Thus experiments
were conducted at Pulham with Sea Scout 14A. The object of these experiments was to
enable an airship to be moored on the lee side of an ordinary wood. The S.S. 14A was
fitted with quick release slips both in the main rigging wires and in the control wires.
The rudder, with its vertical fin, was placed on top of the airship's envelope and the
control wires were carried on tripods round the outside of the envelope. The airship's
car was thus made detachable from the envelope, being wheeled away on a special
chassis. It was then possible to have the envelope 'bagged' down with its underside close
on the ground. Inflated 'bumping bags' were laced to the envelope to prevent the fabric
from chafing on the ground and to hold the envelope valves clear of the ground. When
World War I ended, however, these experiments stopped and this technique of mooring
was never adopted at coastal bases.

But other mooring experiments were of lasting value. I was in this respect surprised
to learn in 1966 that Lord Ventry, the airship authority, while on a visit to Germany
that year, had noted that the Schwab airship kept at Blankensee airport, Lubeck, used
a stub mooring mast 30 ft. high 'based in all essential details on the Scott/Pulham mast
... first used on February 2, 1921, when R.33 arrived from Howden under the late
Flight Lieutenant G. M. Thomas'.

The S.S. 14A, used in 1915 for submarine-spotting in the North Sea and worked from Pulham, had an aeroplane fuselage as its car. Engines to begin with were not that reliable and observers often had to climb out on the undercarriage skid, repair a defect and restart the engine by swinging the propeller with one hand while holding on with the other.

On May 12, 1916, the C.1, a coastal type 'blimp', was taken in tow in Harwich harbour by the light cruiser *Carysfort*. In this way it was hoped to give the Fleet protection which up to then was not possible due to the lack of range of British airships operating from land.

Pulham had a close association with No. 9—the first British rigid craft to take the air. Most of her time, however, was spent elsewhere in experimental mooring and handling tests and on the last of these she was badly damaged. From October 1917, to June, 1918, she lay at Pulham where she was finally dismantled after a mere 198 hours 16 minutes in the air, including 33 hours swinging at a mast.

Airship armament, for use against air and ground targets, was investigated at Pulham because the Admiral Commanding the East Coast had said that such trials could not be conducted over the Wash as they were too dangerous. In January, 1918, tests were made with 2-pounders, a gun being mounted on the top of airship No. 23, resting in an inclined attitude, so that the shots would go into the grass surface. B. N. Wallis, a scientist in the employ of Vickers-Armstrong's, who in later years developed the geodetic form of aircraft construction and the special mine used to breach the German dams in 1943, conducted the Pulham tests but, we are told, none of the test shells were recovered. It was said that they richocheted all over Norfolk.

At one stage, when it was felt that the newest British airships should carry guns, it was decided that the R.33 series should carry one 2-pounder automatic on top for use against other airships. Even 75 mm guns, which were used in aircraft in World War II against ground targets, were contemplated.

Two modern German airships—the L.64 and the L.71—were surrendered to Britain in accordance with the Armistice terms and arrived at Pulham in 1920. However, they made no flying records after their arrival. Mr. Archibald C. Brown, of Bungay, said in 1952 that he visited Pulham on August 5, 1923—a Sunday—and saw three airships in the two sheds. One was the L.71, the others the British R.36 and R.80.

In 1920, as the government looked around for private companies to take over the military airships as passenger carriers, an attempt was made to recruit redundant airship riggers, mechanics, fabric and hydrogen workers for service at Pulham. But the world of commerce was never convinced that the passenger airship had a promising future.

Airstations published their own magazines such as the
Pulham Patrol and Felixstowe's *Wing*.

Mrs L. H. Sheppard

The 644 ft. long R.33, which was often seen at Pulham, was completed in March, 1919, by Armstrong Whitworth and Co. Ltd. to a design prepared by the Admiralty from the wrecks of the L.33 which was forced down at Little Wigborough, Essex, on the night of September 24, 1916, and the L.48 which fell in Suffolk in 1917. The L.33's crew and commander, Kapitanleutnant Bocker, who had often flown over East Anglia, were taken prisoner. The forward gondola of the R.33—her hull had a maximum diameter of 79 ft.—was divided into two sections: in the leading section were the controls and wireless cabinet and in the section behind was an engine. About amidships were two 'wing' gondolas, each containing an engine, and in the stern-most gondola were two other engines which were geared to drive a single large propeller.

An interesting report published by H.M.S.O. in 1921, which I found in a north London secondhand bookshop in the 1950s, describes experiments which were carried out on the R.33 soon after she was completed. The range of the investigation conducted from Pulham on five flights between July and October, 1919, consisted mainly of turning trials at different rudder angles, course with rudders about amidships, deceleration tests from full speed, and petrol consumption trials, with two different sets of airscrews. The forward and two wing propellers were each of 17 ft. 4 ins. diameter in the case of the first set, with the after airscrew 19 ft. 6 ins. in diameter. For the second set the R.33 was fitted with forward and two wing propellers of 16 ft. 8 ins.; the after airscrew remained the same. The R.33 depended on five Sunbeam Maori II engines of 250 h.p. each.

Quite early on in World War I in 1915 the idea of dropping aeroplanes from airships for defence purposes was investigated by Wing Commander N. F. Usborne and Squadron Commander W. P. de Courcy Ireland, who later became commanding

The R 33 at Pulham.    *Suffolk Photo Survey*

Officers at Pulham. Top left. Flight Lieutenant R. F. Montagu, apparently dressed for coping with bees lost his life when the R 38 crashed in 1921. Top right. Major G. H. Scott, commanded R 38 when she became the first airship to make the return flight across the Atlantic in 1919. Died in 1930 when R 101 crashed. Bottom left. Ground officer at Pulham Mr H. J. Brown. Air Commodore E. Maitland lost his life in R 38—bottom right.

W. C. H. Hubbard, H. J. Brown and Mrs L. H. Sheppard

officer at Great Yarmouth. On February 21, 1916, they went aloft in A.P.1, an airborne patrol envelope, for the purpose of flying off her in a B.E.2C biplane. Unfortunately their aircraft became prematurely detached and both airmen were killed.

Fighter defence of airships was examined at Pulham as well. During the summer of 1918 experiments were conducted with the old airship No. 23. Two Sopwith Camels were attached to the underside of her keel and tests were carried out in the shed at Pulham.

Some spectacular experiments were conducted in flight in the Pulham area with the R.33 being used as an aeroplane carrier. Mr. C. H. Kimber, of Harleston, who worked at Pulham in the early days, recalled 'seeing Gloster Gamecock biplanes being dropped from her'.

In the summer of 1918 members of No. 212 Squadron, one of the squadrons at Great Yarmouth, developed the release gear for the carriage of fighters under the new R.33. Later, when the first tests were conducted using a Camel fighter containing a dummy pilot, the aircraft fell away and glided down safely. Then Lieutenant R. E. Keys of 212 Squadron was taken up, released in a Camel, and landed safely at Pulham.

Squadron Leader R. A. de Haga Haig undertook some of these tests, his aeroplane being attached beneath the airship with a main release at the point of balance. Just before release, when the airship was hovering, Squadron Leader Haig climbed down from the airship into the aeroplane. On release the aeroplane fell in a fairly steep dive from which the pilot pulled out. On October 15, 1925, the squadron leader flew off a D.H. 53 monoplane from the R.33. A year later, on October 21, the R.33 carried two Gloster Grebe fighters, one of which was flown off at 2,000 ft. over Pulham by Flying Officer C. Mackenzie-Richards.

Successful hook-ons in mid-air were made by means of a trapeze lowered from the airship. On one occasion Squadron Leader Haig fouled the trapeze, smashed the D.H. 53's propeller, and had to glide down.

With these experiments complete it was felt that the airship in war might become an aerial aircraft carrier. Certainly the United States went on to make airships carry several fighters at a time. Then the technique was dropped. However, after the 1939-1945 war the U.S.A.F. carried out experiments in which a jet fighter was carried in the bomb bay of a giant B-36 aircraft and released on the lines of the Pulham tests of years earlier.

On the morning of April 16, 1925, the R.33 found herself moored at Pulham in a terrific westerly gale with 50 m.p.h. gusts. At 9.50 a.m. the mooring arm, due to defective material, broke and the airship's nose came in contact with the mast head, in the process of which No. 1 gas bag was punctured and the nose smashed. Flight Lieutenant (later Wing Commander) Ralph S. Booth, who died in 1969, the airship's first officer,

1

2

3

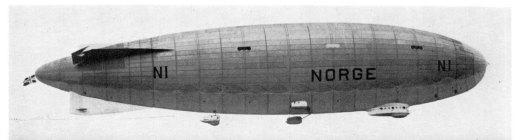

4

5

6

1) C 26. Note gun platform on top of her envelope. 2) R 26 first flew on March 20, 1918. 3) R 34 at Pulham. 4) *Norge*, acquired by Roald Amundsen for his 1926 expedition to the North Pole, visited Pulham. 5) R 36 moored at Pulham. 6) R 101 of which the detail design and manufacture of her entire hull structure was carried out by Boulton and Paul.   *C. L. Elliott, W. H. H. Hubbard and George Swain*

at once took command of the skeleton crew, jettisoned ballast from the forepart, and got the R.33's nose clear of the mast. Within two minutes one of the engines was started, followed shortly by the remaining four. As the crew wrestled to bring the airship under control those of her crew left on the ground at Pulham knew that she had enough fuel and oil for a two days' voyage and food for three days.

Squadron Leader Brown, whose two daughters 'grew up in airships' at Pulham, was at the time getting the men's wages from the bank at Harleston when his driver reported: 'The ship has broken away'. The driver wanted to chase it in the station car, but Squadron Leader Brown quietly assured him that the damaged R.33 would ride out the storm and then return—to Pulham. As things turned out he was right. Over the village of Starston the airship was seen to turn, as if trying to return to Pulham, but she lost leeway and was soon lost in low cloud.

News of the R.33's plight was quickly flashed to the coast. At 10.21 a.m. the airship crossed near Lowestoft. At 10.40 a.m. the local lifeboat, with Coxswain Arthur Spurgeon at the wheel, set out after the airship. H.M.S. *Godetia,* the fishery protection gun boat, under Commander F. W. D. Twigg, also put out. The lifeboat was under sail and motor power, but the wind increased, and the sails had to be taken off. The last Coxswain Spurgeon saw of the R.33 she was about 1,000 ft. up, and eight miles away. The lifeboat continued to follow until the airship was about 14 miles from land when, due to a sharp rain storm, contact was lost. Meanwhile, H.M.S. *Godetia* continued to chase the R.33.

Hundreds of volunteers at Pulham help to haul down the crippled R 33 after her epic flight in 1925.
George Swain

At about 3 p.m. on April 16 the airship was off the Dutch coast, steering in a north easterly direction. She had been told to do this by the Air Ministry so that, by the evening, she would be able to return with a following wind. By 5 p.m. she was 120 miles from Pulham and riding the storm gallantly. Every 15 minutes the R.33's wireless operator, Mr. S. T. Keeley, sent out a message, thus enabling the Waalhaven, (Holland), Croydon and Pulham radio stations to locate her position by means of wireless direction finders. At Diss an amateur radio enthusiast was able to listen in to the aerial drama. High over the Dutch coast, somewhere between Ymuiden and Zandvoort, the R.33 started hovering from 8.44 p.m. until about 5 a.m. on April 17. It was a great moment back at Pulham when Mr. Keeley radioed: 'Returning to England'. Shortly after 1 p.m. the crippled airship, whose torn nose had been temporarily closed by lashing down the flapping fabric, was sighted off Covehithe.

Soon the R.33 was back over East Anglian soil and, as she neared Pulham, her crew saw people streaming along the roads and lanes leading to the air station. More than 300 men and boys were formed into a landing party. As the victorious airship descended over Pulham, with her bow looking as if it had hit a wall, cheers echoed across the heath. Through a megaphone Flight Lieutenant H. C. Irwin, who had been in command of the R.33 before she broke away, controlled the landing party. Others who had ridden out the storm aboard the R.33 were: Flight Sergeant G. W. Hunt, Messrs. C. B. Oliver, G. E. Long, L. H. Rowe, R. W. Mayes, J. Walkinshaw, G. Watts, G. V. Bell, L. A. Moncrieff, R. W. Dick, J. E. Scott, G. N. Potter, S. E. Scott, N. G. Mann, L. H. King, W. R. Gent, Z. Little and J. E. Rarp. By 3.50 p.m., 30 minutes after her descent, the R.33 was housed safely in the hangar alongside the R.36. Major George H. Scott, who was in charge at Pulham, described the flight as one of the greatest achievements in airships either in Great Britain, America or Germany. . . . The R.33 had been in the air for close on 30 hours. King George V later gave presentation watches to the entire crew. Repairs to the R.33 lasted from May to August, 1925, when a new nose cone was finally fitted on August 18.

After the epic flight of the R.33 an enterprising local miller perpetuated the deed on his flour bags. Mr. W. S. Kirby on behalf of Walter Green & Sons Ltd., Castle Flour Mills, Beccles, told me: 'At that time this firm supplied flour to a baker, Mr. A. Rice Cattermole, Pulham St. Mary. who packed it in 3 lb. bags, on which was printed an airship picture of the R.33 moored to the mast with the words "Tested and tried" '. Mr. Charles L. Elliott, who spent his boyhood in the Pulham area, said he had heard that the miller concerned did not think much of the slogan 'Tested and tried' because the R.33 came back 'tattered and torn'. However, Mr. Cattermole replied that his bags often did so, too, and he was rather proud of the trademark.

Local papers sometimes reported the peace time sighting of airships. Thus the *Eastern Daily Press* on August 11, 1919, noted: 'On Saturday afternoon a large airship, gleaming in the sun, passed over Yarmouth and proceeded seawards. At 5.0 p.m. an airship, which may have been the same, was seen between Yarmouth and Caister, travelling in a north westerly direction. Just before 6 p.m. an airship of a smaller type appeared over the north end of the town so low that her number S.R.1 could be plainly read, and she travelled south in a line almost parallel with the parade'.

When World War I ended British airship designers, impressed with the promising achievements of the war years, turned their attention to the development of transoceanic commercial airships. To the R.34, sister ship of the R.33 which was built from a detailed study of crashed Zeppelins, went the distinction in 1919 of the first flight return across the Atlantic by an airship. She set out from East Fortune, Midlothian, Scotland, on July 2 and reached Roosevelt Field, Mineola, Long Island, New York, 108 hours later. Over the coast of Ireland, on the outward trip, a stowaway was discovered. During preparations to land in America, it was realised that nobody on the ground seemed able to direct operations, so an officer of the airship, Flight Lieutenant J. E. M. Pritchard, parachuted down and hastily instructed an improvised ground crew in the art of securing an airship. On July 13, a Sunday, the R.34, with Major George H. Scott in command, came back in 75 hours three minutes, the airship flying to Pulham because of bad weather in the north. With him was Air Commodore Edward Maitland*, who in 1916 was appointed commanding officer of Pulham and a year later Superintendent of Airships. The landing party at Pulham consisted of 500 to 600 men, including some from aerodromes at East Harling and Norwich plus a considerable muster of discharged soldiers in civilian dress. After making two slow circles of Pulham the R.34, with seven officers and 25 ratings aboard, signalled that she was ready to be assisted down. So that this was possible long trailing ropes were released from her forepart. Colonel W. N. Hensley, jnr., of the U.S. Army, who was aboard, said: 'The whole day Friday we did not know our position. We could not get a shot at the sun, moon or stars. We were travelling in fog with water dripping over us.' The R.34, which was lost in a mooring accident in 1921, was played into Pulham after her Atlantic flight by the station band, the pieces being 'The Call of Duty' and 'See the Conquering Hero Comes'. Is there much to remember the R.34 by today? Well, she carried a little mail on her return to this country. It was stamped with an ordinary type of postmark which, however, included the title R.34. The envelopes, I understand, change hands from time to time at quite high prices. Then, in 1962, a scale model of the R.34 was handed over to the nation at a reception at London Airport.

On April 21, 1926, a Sunday, large crowds gathered at Pulham to watch the arrival of the airship 'Norge', designed by General Umberto Nobile, which had been acquired for Roald Amundsen's expedition to the North Pole. She was overhead at 3 p.m., dropping ballast, but atmospheric disturbances made it inadvisable to land before five. The 'Norge' was placed alongside the R.33 in the hangar at Pulham, and her crew were glad of a night's rest after their 32 hour flight from Italy. On April 13, with weather conditions ideal, the visitor left. A special hangar had been made for the 'Norge' at King's Bay, Spitsbergen. In 1954 Miss A. M. Kay, of St.-Anne's on Sea,

*Air Commodore Maitland, who was killed in the disaster to the R.38 on August 24, 1921, made a large number of descents from aircraft of all descriptions, balloon, kite balloon, airship and aeroplane, to convince others of the importance of the parachute in saving life.

Lancashire, who once visited the famous hangar, sent me cloth and rope from the structure, souvenirs which must have seen brave men. About 16 miles of beams were required for the framework of the hangar and about 12,000 square yards of canvas to cover its sides and gables. On May 12, 1926, the Pole was reached and the 'Norge', despite fog, icing and a gale, went on to land safely in Alaska.

Nevil Shute (N.S. Norway), who wrote *Slide Rule,* was another well known name associated with Pulham. Writing of the final test flight of the R.100 in January, 1930, he said: 'On enquiring where we were, I was told that we were passing over Lowestoft. I asked what we had come there for, and I was told that since the wife of Steff, third officer, came from Lowestoft we had come as a graceful compliment . . .' Steff, unfortunately, died in the R.101.

An unusual airship memorial can be seen in the Roman Catholic Church of the Holy Family and St. Michael at Kesgrave, near Ipswich. The church was built in memory of Squadron Leader Michael Rope who was killed when the R.101 crashed near Beauvais, France, on October 5, 1930, while on a flight to India. All but seven of the 53 people on board, the cream of Britain's aeronautical world, lost their lives when the airship, after encountering a violent rain storm, struck the side of a hill and burst into flames. The dead included Lord Thompson, Secretary of State for Air, Air Vice Marshal Sir William Sefton Brancker, Director of Civil Aviation, who shortly before had attended that year's Suffolk Aero Club ball, and Major Scott, well known at

Memorial Church at Kesgrave built in 1931 in memory of Squadron Leader Michael Rope who died when R 101 crashed at Beauvais in France in 1930.   *Mrs Doreen Rope*

R 33 being fitted with a new nose cone. *Suffolk Photo Survey*

Pulham, who had made the first double crossing of the Atlantic by air in 1919 in the R.34. The crash of the R.101, with its heavy loss of life, ended any further development of the airship in Great Britain. When the church was built at Kesgrave metal was used from the wreck of the R.101. Hanging from the roof is a perfect scale model of the airship in which Squadron Leader Rope lost his life.

Shortly after the crash of the R.101, Sir Samuel Hoare, in a letter to *The Times,* said of the crew: 'When I flew with them, I marked the rare balance between brain and hand and eye that their airmanship displayed . . . now they have died together, and with them has gone a great treasure of gathered knowledge and invaluable experience'.

Mrs. Doreen Rope, the widow of Squadron Leader Rope, told me: 'We built the little church in 1931, and had an extension built in 1955 . . . Small pieces of the airship metal were worked into door handles and the like. The Ropes are a Suffolk family, farmers mostly, though my husband's father as a man moved to Shrewsbury where he was a doctor'.

144

Robert Higham in his book *The British Rigid Airship* 1908-1931, in referring to the team responsible for the building of the R.101, said: 'Squadron Leader Rope who designed the parachute wiring of the gasbags has been described as close to genius'.

Incidentally, the crew of the R.101, (the airship cost £777,000 to build), was entirely composed of civilians with the exception of two officers and an N.C.O. of the R.A.F., one of the officers being Squadron Leader Rope. He had been aboard the ill-fated R.38 on all but her last trip on August 24, 1921, when over the Humber she broke her back and crashed, killing nearly all the crew. Another East Anglian member of the crew of the R.38, Yoxford born Mr. W. A. Potter, the assistant chief coxswain, also died in the R.101.

The Norwich firm of Boulton and Paul, whose contribution to aviation has already been described at length, had a part in the making of the R.101. It was the company's experience in metal construction, and particularly in the handling of stainless steels, which was a deciding factor in its selection, in 1927, to collaborate with the Royal Airship Works in the design and construction of this airship. Of five million cubic feet capacity, the R.101 was very much larger than any previous dirigible but departed entirely from former practice in that steel was used for the main structure members of the frame instead of duralumin. The detail design and manufacture of the entire main hull structure was carried out by Boulton and Paul, and Mr. North, whose brilliant work was mentioned earlier on, acted during that period as consultant to the Director of Airship Development.

H. F. King, in a tribute to the Norwich firm's achievements in a special article in *Flight* for July 8, 1955, said of this work: 'The great size of the ship and the multiplicity of frame members obliged the Boulton and Paul engineers to go to extraordinary lengths in the calculation of sizes of individual members to avoid cumulative errors and in the accurate setting of assembly jigs to suit. So meticulously was this pursued that, when the frame was erected at Cardington, every component went into place without the slightest hitch. The tragic loss of the great airship was in no way a reflection on its structural design or manufacture'.

Living at Pulham St. Mary in 1969 were two men with memories of the airship days. Mr. Guy Palmer was one of the men employed by Smith of Bunwell, the contractors who worked on the construction of Pulham airship station when more permanent structures were put up. Then there was Mr. Walter Hubbard who began work at Pulham in April, 1919, and was one of the landing party when the R.34 ended her double crossing of the Atlantic later that year. He said in 1969: 'I think the development of the airship might have gone much further than it did if there had not been so many tragedies'. But Mr. Hubbard probably did not know that in 1969 plans were going ahead for a German airship with nuclear power, costing about £15m, to be known as the ALV-1.

CHAPTER X

How the Airports Grew

THE SUFFOLK AERO CLUB was founded in 1925 by Mr. Courtney N. Prentice, an ex-R.F.C. bomber pilot, of Ipswich, and operated from Hadleigh for several years. Later his son, Mr. Eugene C. M. Prentice, of Harkstead, ran the West Suffolk Aero Club from Bury St. Edmunds and then from Ipswich.

Mr. Eugene Prentice learnt to fly in 1936 and flew as a Flight Captain in the Air Transport Auxiliary in the last war, his war time flying time as aircraft captain being 1,767 hours. His total hours flying as aircraft captain stands at the time of writing at 2,939 hours.

Mr. Prentice told me: 'My first trip was in 1924 in an Avro 504K from Bucklesham belonging to Berkshire Aviation Tours, complete with the traditional "toothpick" and driven by a Le Clerget rotary engine. The whole awesome affair, I was five at the time, was painted in red and silver and smelt strongly of castor oil'.

By all accounts the Prentice family, who have links with Suffolk going back more than five generations, were interested in aviation at an early stage. For in *Flight* for April 6, 1912, a picture was published of Miss Dorothy Prentice, elder sister of Mr. Courtney Prentice, being instructed on a Bleriot. She must have been among the small band of pioneer women aviators who were learning to fly at Hendon in 1912, for on June 29, 1912, some of the women pilots were competent enough to take part in the first ladies' air race to be held in this country. Miss Prentice, it was recorded at the time, was a keen student of aeronautics. She learnt to fly at the same time as Baroness Schenck, a young German woman, who was taught on a Howard-Wright biplane.

Miss Prentice, like the rest of the young ladies of those days who had pilot aspirations, was often mentioned in the press. *The Outfitter* in 1911-1912 addressed the following letter to Miss Prentice when she was at the Ewen Flying School, Hendon: 'That you should have found feminine attire unsuitable for anyone seriously taking up flying, is not surprising, and it seems quite appropriate to the pursuit, that, in common with the male pupils of the school, you should wear trousers. We cannot, however, pretend to say we admire the costume in which the *Daily Mirror* photograph presents you to the readers of that journal. Surely feminine ingenuity in time will create a flying costume, which should be artistic as well as practical. Ever since we made the acquaintance of the "Flying Men and Women" in the romance of Peter Wilkins, we have been waiting for the arrival of the Flying Lady. Our trade, of course, will open a special department for her requirements'. Today this early pioneer among women aviators lives at Leiston. Her name is Mrs. Dorothy Banks-Warner.

Among the famous airwomen who were members of the old Suffolk Aero Club were Lady Bailey, their president, and Miss Winifred Spooner. In 1929 Lady Bailey,

First members of the Suffolk Aero Club, Hadleigh 1929. _Mrs J. Courtney Prentice_

who was born in 1890 and learnt to fly in 1927, became the first woman to win the Britannia Challange Trophy, the most coveted prize of British aviation and awarded annually to the British aviator who, in the opinion of an expert committee, accomplished the most meritorious performance in the air during the year. For her win Lady Bailey, who flew in many air races and competitions in England, made a remarkable solo flight from England to South Africa and back, a distance of 18,000 miles, in a D.H. Moth light aeroplane between March 9, 1928, and January 16, 1929.

Born in 1900, Miss Spooner, who died in 1933 following an illness which lasted only a day, was at the time of her death definitely the only woman in Britain earning a regular living as the personal pilot of a private owner of machines. Like Miss Dorothy N. Spicer, who is mentioned elsewhere, she made a study of the technical side as well, so that when she was flying abroad she was her own mechanic.

The Hon. Mrs. Victor Bruce based her Bluebird IV G-ABDS at Ipswich in readiness for an attempt on the world's endurance record.

The club, to begin with, had as its chief instructor Mr. George E. Lowdell, an ex-R.A.F. sergeant pilot, who was a skilled handler of the popular Avro 504 trainer.

Later he joined Brooklands School of Flying but paid weekly visits to the club. By 1928 the Suffolk Aero Club had three Blackburn Bluebird two seater biplanes—the first light two seater to go into production with side-by-side seating instead of a tandem arrangement. A year later another branch of the club had been opened at Conington, near Cambridge, using two more Bluebirds. As a result of the regular Hadleigh-Cambridge repositioning flights a passenger service (one per aircraft) was available between these two places. The so-called Ipswich-Cambridge Airway charged 30s. single or 50s. return on their Monday and Thursday flights. There was also a flight to Grantham, Lincolnshire, on a Tuesday to connect with the Flying Scotsman.

In 1931, when the Suffolk Aero Club was reorganised at Ipswich, the Bluebirds were sold and replaced by two Robinson Redwing biplanes with Genet engines. Soon a branch of the club was opened at Colchester with Bluebird G-ABNP generally operating from there, while Bluebird G-ABMU mostly flew from Ipswich. By the end of 1932 the Redwing Aircraft Co. had moved to Colchester. Redwing G-ABRM, which had refinements such as navigation lights, was a Colchester-built machine and started operating from Ipswich in the following year. Other club machines, often seen at Ipswich in the 1930s, were a Miles Hawk and a Klemn Swallow—an extremely safe, low wing monoplane of German design, built under licence in this country.

The Suffolk Aero Club by 1928 had three Blackburn Bluebird two seater biplanes. Members were photographed at Hadleigh about this time.   *E. C. M. Prentice*

Ipswich aerodrome, once described as having a deafening chorus of larks in summer, was officially opened by the Duke of Windsor, then Prince of Wales, on June 26, 1930, when he visited the town to attend the Wolsey Pageant—the corporate tribute of Ipswich to Cardinal Thomas Wolsey who was born there in the 15th century. The Duke flew in escorted by four service aircraft, and before the ceremony he went to the local aero club house to remove his flying kit. Then, in the presence of Lady· Bailey, president of the Suffolk Aero Club, he congratulated Ipswich on its far-sighted policy in establishing the aerodrome.

The new terminal buildings at Ipswich were not opened officially until Saturday, July 9, 1930, Suffolk Air Day, when Captain Harold Balfour, Parliamentary Under Secretary of State for Air, attended. However, no important building work was done at the aerodrome until the Straight Corporation, about which I shall shortly have more to say, was entrusted with its management in February, 1936. At the Suffolk Air Day there was a full military and civil display of flying, including a high speed run by Mr. (later Sir Giles) Guthrie, one time chairman of B.O.A.C. and then a member of the Ipswich Aero Club, in his 240 m.p.h. Percival Mew Gull racer.

The founder and governing director of the Straight Corporation was Mr. Whitney Straight, who was born in New York in 1912, his interest in flying having started when he was seven. His family in America was associated with aviation, for his first cousin, C. V. Whitney, was chairman of Pan-American Airways. Later Whitney Straight settled in England and went to Trinity College, Cambridge, at the same time keeping his private aeroplane at Marshall's Flying School. He established a number of flying schools in this country, including one at Ipswich, and could claim to control Clacton airport. The schools were under the direction and personal supervision of Captain W. N. Cumming, formerly of Imperial Airways Ltd., who carried out the first long range tests of the Empire flying boat 'Caledonia' which was seen off the East Coast in 1937.

Mr. Whitney Straight, from the very beginning of his business career, had progressive ideas about airports, he had studied some in Germany, and he believed that an aerodrome, in addition to receiving aeroplanes, had a duty to provide facilities for the public to watch the activities in comfort not only because this was a useful source of aerodrome revenue but also because it helped to make people airminded.

From 1938 onwards, as the fear of war increased, Ipswich airport undertook Army co-operation flying in the early evening in connection with the Observer Corps, as well as night flying contracts for areas close to Norwich and Weybourne near Cromer. Sometimes as many as nine aeroplanes were needed simultaneously at night. The Norwich and Weybourne contracts involved flying at specified heights and courses over a roughly oval area covering perhaps 200 square miles of country. Navigation lights were switched off, and the searchlights did their best to find the machines. The Observer Corps work involved flying at a given ground speed over a prescribed and roughly rectangular course.

Miss Dorothy Prentice learnt to fly at Hendon in 1912. Her flying suit was discussed in the press at that time.

Mrs J. Courtney Prentice

A passenger, carried on one of these flights, noted in the July, 1938, edition of *Straightaway:* 'The course to Norwich lies over open country and, at night more than by day, one realises the quiet of these Eastern counties. Car lights were few, and it was apparently past bedtime in farms and cottages. Though it was night on the ground, the sky was still comparatively light, and held traces of the sunset. Black, streaky clouds fringed the horizon without ever appearing to come any nearer, and above it was clear dark blue with stars appearing, first a few and then the whole outfit'.

'Arrived over Norwich, we started our patrol at 4,000 ft., climbing at stated intervals to 6,000 and 8,000 . . . Six searchlights switched on, waved about and almost at once we were caught and held in a beam. The others converged on us, and we had a glimmer of the trapped sensation which must be familiar to fighting pilots . . .'.

War was in the air: soon those same searchlights were to seek out enemy raiders flying against East Anglia and, on other occasions, point here and then there to guide lost or crippled R.A.F. aircraft to safety.

Civil Air Guard training started at Ipswich airport in October, 1938, and an R.A.F. volunteer reserve training school was specially built to meet the training requirements of rearmament. It was completed and opened in 1939.

East Anglia's desire to be first in the field was illustrated in 1938 when Mr. Courtney Prentice, of Prentice Air Services, Ipswich, became sole concessionaire in this country for the American Taylorcraft. This light aircraft, a high wing monoplane, sold in the United States for about £300 and here for just over £450.

At this time Mr. Courtney Prentice, who by 1946 had flown 3,000 hours, founded the West Suffolk Aero Club on the Newmarket Road at Bury St. Edmunds. This aerodrome, like Ipswich, was also municipally owned. The new club operated three Lycoming engined Taylorcraft. A Piper Cub completed the 'fleet' and for instructional purposes was the most popular of all. The first chief flying instructor at Bury St. Edmunds was the late Wing Commander Bruce Lockhart, Mr. Eugene Prentice taking over from him in March, 1939.

In the 1930s all the aero engines used by the Straight Corporation and allied companies, at an early stage they operated 40 aircraft, were sent to Ipswich airport for overhaul. The workshops were small but efficient, pride in individual workmanship being encouraged. Sometimes aircraft were flown in to have their engines attended to; sometimes aero engines were delivered in crates to Ipswich station for transport to the work-shops. The Straight Corporation left Ipswich in September, 1939, when the government requisitioned the airport facilities, it being noted in official records that on September 6, 1939,* 48 hours after the R.A.F. had made the first bombing attack of the war from Suffolk, 13 aircraft from Wattisham, which had sent aircraft against the enemy, were dispersed to Ipswich Airport.

Today Ipswich airport continues with its flying connections. And, despite the long service, the small metal hangars alongside Maryon Road, which were once used at Hadleigh when the Suffolk Aero Club was established in the 1920s, are still in use. Round about there are other reminders that Ipswich has not forgotten the world of

*A version of this is that on September 1, 1939, Ipswich airport was taken over by 110 Squadron and that on September 4 a flight of five Blenheims took off from Ipswich to join other aircraft in the first bombing raid of the war.

Mr and Mrs Courtney N. Prentice seen at Ipswich airport in 1937 with their son, Eugene C. M. Prentice, and his Piper Cub.
Eugene C. M. Prentice

In its heyday Ipswich airport was a model of sound planning and well in advance of its contemporaries.

Airways Union Ltd.

aviation, for there are road, close and crescent names like Lindbergh, Cobham, Bader, Wright, Cranwell and Halton.

The Norfolk and Norwich Aero Club, which now uses the old R.A.F. station at Swanton Morley as its airfield, was founded in 1927 and was the 'first light aeroplane club to be promoted by the civic heads of a municipality'. Their first aircraft, a Moth, was given by Mr. Henry N. Holmes, who was later knighted, the club's first president, and Mr. James Hardy.

When the Norfolk and Norwich Aero Club was founded in 1927, here it is interesting to remember that Norwich in the Great War had been a productive aircraft centre, it adopted as part of its policy the promotion and development of the airport at Mousehold to the north of the city. At that time the idea of air travel becoming part and parcel of civic life was regarded by many citizens as unlikely for many years.

The Norfolk and Norwich Aero Club, which had pupils from Canada, South America, Australia, New Zealand and even China, started off in a humble way and equipment was meagre. It is recorded that their solitary aircraft of the early days had a variety of experiences being subjected to one or two minor crashes and, on one occasion, suffered the ordeal of being towed through the city with folded wings to be displayed in the market place to encourage the citizens generally to take an interest in this new form of transport. Hundreds of free flights were given in the early days in an effort to make the city and county air minded.

Preserved today in the Norfolk and Norwich Record Office are the log book and aviator's certificate No. 8250 of the Royal Aero Club for a typical pupil of the time, Mr. Hector C. Mack, of Place Farm, Drayton, Norwich, who started a flying course at Mousehold in June, 1927, on D.H. 60 G-EBQX. He went solo just a year later.

In 1932 the municipality of Norwich, encouraged by the Air Ministry, decided to acquire the aerodrome and develop it as an airport. In this work the Corporation co-operated with the aero club, and an existing World War I hangar was turned into a presentable club house. It even had covered tennis and squash courts.

A taxi service by club planes was provided, while Mr. F. Leo Crilly, managing director of Crilly Airways, who first realised the possibilities of Norwich becoming an important airport, established an airline which had daily services to Leicester, Bristol, Liverpool, Nottingham and Northampton. Another service, that of aerial photography, was also provided at Mousehold and proved useful to commercial houses, estate agents and archaeologists. Gliding was also encouraged.

Norwich airport, which attracted many famous names in British aviation, was opened by the Prince of Wales on June 21, 1933. The visitors' book for the club, incidentally, records no fewer than seven Royal signatures. Royal visits to the Norfolk and Norwich Aero Club were made by the Prince of Wales (May 30, 1928, and April 21, 1933), Prince George (June 7, 1930, May 2, 1932, and May 19, 1934), Prince Henry (May 19, 1934), and Princess Marina (July 8, 1934).

Early in 1934 Mr. Harold Birchall, who was one of the first pilots to be trained by the club, was given permission to put into operation a scheme of his for training schoolboys over 17 to fly. In August, 1934, the first public schools' aviation camp was held at Mousehold, and all seven pupils got their licences.

The opening of Norwich airport was an occasion to remember. As the Prince of Wales stepped from his personal aircraft, a D.H. Dragon, he was greeted by the Lord

The Prince of Wales greeted by the Lord Mayor of Norwich, Ald. H. N. Holmes, when he arrived to open the Norwich airport in 1933.   *George Swain*

Norwich photographed from the air in 1921.

Mayor of Norwich (Mr. Henry N. Holmes), his Sheriffs, and by Lieutenant Colonel F. C. Shelmerdine, Director of Civil Aviation. Boulton Paul Sidestrands of No. 101 Squadron were lined up at Mousehold, and the Royal visitor also inspected the Fairey (Napier) Long Range Monoplane which was described to him by two long distance pioneers, Squadron Leader Oswald R. Gayford and Flight Lieutenant G. E. Nicholetts.

Flying charges* for the period make interesting reading today. In May, 1935, one could have *ab initio* dual instruction at Norwich for 35s. an hour, refresher dual for 25s., and solo dual for a similar charge. Gipsy Moth types were used. Charges for the Fox Moth were equally modest: solo and one passenger 30s. an hour, with two passengers 35s. Furthermore, said the club's booklet of rules and regulations, 'All these charges include, where relevant, cost of instruction, petrol and oil, damage to aircraft in excess of £5 and third party insurance'.

Aerial photography, as I have said, was worked from Mousehold. In this connection Mr. George Swain, F.I.B.P., F.R.P.S., F.R.S.A., the Norwich photographer, started aerial photography in 1920 with Frank Neale as pilot, their mount being an Avro 504K.

Of Frank Neale, Mr. Swain recalled: 'Mr. Bollonds, his mechanic, used to walk the wings, wearing plimsolls, and on one occasion I saw him do a hand-stand on the top wing—he seemed to be leaning on the wind. Some people will not believe this, but he did so. Neale's partner was Summerfield. Bollonds was quite a character. He rode a direct belt drive single geared Norton motor cycle capable then of well over 60 m.p.h.'

*In the course of looking at original papers owned by a famous Martlesham Heath test pilot, who started flying at Hendon before World War I, cross country flights in 1913 were expensive—for instance, from Hendon to Brooklands return—a distance of 38 miles—cost £26 5s.

Just as the early pilots learnt from hard experience, so did Mr. Swain his aerial photography. 'My first aerial camera', said Mr. Swain, 'was a converted T.P. Reflex which I found very useful because it had no bellows to be blown in by the slipstream. My very first photographs were a mixed lot as I overlooked the vibration of the aircraft and at times braced myself tightly by resting my elbows on the cockpit side, transmitting the vibrations to the camera'.

Mousehold waited for an unusual visitor one day in 1936, but his descent was prevented by windy conditions. Crowds gathered in anticipation of seeing Clem Sohn, the 'Bird Man', drop with wings attached to his arms before opening his parachute. For his famous stunt Sohn, an American, wore two wings, two parachutes and carried a canister of chemical powder to enable spectators to follow his evolutions. Sohn lost his life at Vincennes, France, in 1937.

Captain A. A. Rice, as chairman of the Norfolk and Norwich Aero Club in 1954, told the *Eastern Daily Press*: 'At the outbreak of war the club had trained about 300 pilots. Many were destined to achieve great fame in the R.A.F. Others are still flying with the airlines of the world . . . There was . . . Group Captain Dennis Gilham, D.S.O., D.F.C., A.F.C., and Wing Commander Ralph Mottram, D.F.C. and bar (son of the ex-Lord Mayor), both of whom were trained by the Norfolk and Norwich Aero Club as schoolboys'.

Captain Rice told me: 'Incidentally, our very first woman to go solo (although she didn't ultimately qualify owing to being a cripple) was Mrs. Anne Cator (nee Cayley) of the family of Sir George Cayley, the Yorkshire air pioneer'. Mrs. Cator, who was the great great grand daughter of the air pioneer, was the mother of Mr. John Cator of Woodbastwick Hall, Norwich.

Marshall's (Cambridge) Ltd., whose aerodrome works and facilities changed Cambridge from a purely university town, was founded in 1909 as a garage business by Mr. David Marshall, the present managing director's father, Mr. Arthur Marshall, at Jesus Lane in the centre of Cambridge. In 1926 the son of founder learnt to fly and decided that there 'seemed to be some future in the aviation business'.

At that time the Marshall family lived in a house on the Newmarket road roughly where Quainton Close is situated. Beside the house, stretching down to where the Abbey football ground now is, were fields, and in 1929 Mr. Marshall bought a second-hand Handley Page bomber for £5 and established Marshall's Flying School Ltd. on the site in the same year. Within a few years the original site proved too small, and in 1938 the company moved to the present site of some 640 acres, at which time the buildings consisted of Nos. 1 and 2 hangars, the control building and administration block, garage and one or two odd stores.

CHAPTER XI

The 1930s

IN THE 1930s north Norfolk saw two well known women aviators, Miss Pauline Gower and Miss Dorothy N. Spicer, flying business men and holidaymakers across the Wash from Hunstanton to Skegness. Starting with one aeroplane and living in an old gypsy caravan beside their aircraft, which they maintained themselves, they worked up a flourishing air taxi service. Incidentally, by June, 1935, Miss Spicer had become the first woman in the world to hold ground engineers' licences A, B, C, and D, enabling her to build aeroplanes and engines and to approve the materials required for the work. A contemporary of Amy Johnson, Miss Spicer, and her husband, Flight Lieutenant Richard Pearse, were killed in an aircraft accident in 1946.

The two aviators spent their first summer in Norfolk in 1933, renting a field just outside Hunstanton. They used to start carrying passengers about 10.30 a.m. each day and, by all accounts, they had several odd clients. One night Miss Gower and Miss Spicer, having gone to bed, were approached by a couple who did their utmost to persuade Miss Gower to take them for a moonlight flight over Sandringham. Was it a plot to bomb the royal house? Well, no one ever knew because the prudent aviators, despite the offer of good money, never made that flight by moonlight. In order to get publicity without making noise over Hunstanton, in those days the police would not allow noise over a town, the two pilots arranged with the proprietor of a speedboat to allow their passengers to aim small flour bags at the boat as it sped along. The 'bombing' event, while the speedboat swerved about, attracted crowds on the front at Hunstanton. Another advertising stunt, as the aviators had to contend with a thriving South Beach fair, was the painting under the fuselage of the words 'Cheap Flights'. They even offered a trip lasting for about a minute and a half for 3s. 6d. A 5s. flight involved a circuit of Hunstanton. The return trip from Hunstanton to Skegness cost £1. On bank holidays and good days in August Miss Gower and Miss Spicer took a little over £30, and this meant taking between 150 and 200 passengers.

It was during their first summer at Hunstanton that a certain Bruce Williams suggested that the show could be improved if they let him be a stunt parachutist. He lived near the field, and did parachute drops on Sundays and holidays. On the last day of their 1934 tour the two women pilots staged a special show at Hunstanton with their blue Spartan. Williams did a delayed drop from 3,000 ft. and only just escaped death when his parachute failed to open at a safe height, in fact, it developed about 100 ft. above the ground. In his second jump that day he fell into a field containing donkeys. On the third jump of the afternoon he was blown into the middle of the watching crowd. But the worst flight the Hunstanton spectators experienced, not that day, however, was when Williams landed on the King's Lynn-Hunstanton railway line a second or two behind the last carriage of a train as it went by.

Born in 1894, Sir Alan Cobham, the celebrated British pilot, who by his early survey flights and air publicity campaigns stirred Britain between the wars into a more air minded nation, was seen a number of times in East Anglia in the 1930s when he organised tours by National Aviation Day Ltd. (1932-1933) and displays by National Aviation Displays Ltd. (1934-35). Among the aircraft he used was a D.H. 61 Giant Moth called 'Youth of Britain' in which he did a 21 week tour of the country. On December 2, 1969, Sir Alan, who is chairman of Flight Refuelling Ltd., of Wimborne, Dorset, and a pioneer of air-to-air refuelling, presented a trophy at R.A.F. Marham to R.A.F. Strike Command to be competed for annually by squadrons in the command's Tanker Force which refuels military aircraft in flight.

In 1970 Sir Alan gave me a list of his calling places in East Anglia during the period 1932 to 1935. In 1932 it was Cromer (July 22), Norwich (July 23), Great Yarmouth (July 24), Ipswich (July 25), and Cambridge (October 11). In 1933 it was Ipswich (May 27), Cambridge (June 1), Cromer (August 16-17), Lowestoft (August 18), Norwich (August 19), Great Yarmouth (August 20), Ely (September 26) and Bungay (September 27). In 1934 it was Gorleston (August 30), Cromer (August 31), Hunstanton (September 1), and Ely (September 11). In 1935 it was Cambridge (June 20), Ipswich (June 22), Felixstowe (July 10), Southwold (July 11), Cromer (July 12), Norwich (July 13) and Great Yarmouth (July 14). It was at Ipswich aerodrome in 1935, after days of expectation, that I had the chance of a flight with Sir Alan, who was taking up parties of youngsters, but I declined at the last moment, the reason being that I felt I should not find my parents when we landed.

During his tours of East Anglia, Sir Alan Cobham made use of any suitable landing area and, for example, at Bungay he selected Carlton House Farm.

When, on November 20, 1924, Sir Alan Cobham set out on the first of his remarkable series of long distance survey flights, from London to Rangoon and back he covered the 17,000 miles without a forced landing. This he said was due to his engineer, Mr. Arthur B. Elliott, who had Feltwell connections, whose skill and care released the pilot from all engine worry during the 220 hours of flying time. Although born at Brixton Hill, London, Elliott as a boy spent much of his time with his grandparents, Mr. and Mrs. Isaac Lyons, at Feltwell Lodge, for his mother was a native of the village. The boy Elliott went to Feltwell Elementary School and attended St. Mary's Sunday School.

On June 30, 1926, with only one companion, his trusted engineer, Elliott, Sir Alan Cobham took off in a seaplane from Rochester, Kent, on his great London to Australia return flight. It was while flying down the Tigris to Bushire, on the Persian Gulf, that tragedy intervened while they were flying low for navigation reasons. Suddenly there was 'a violent and alarming explosion', and Elliott passed out a leaf from his message pad saying he had been wounded. Sir Alan Cobham decided to make for Basra, so that Elliott could be treated by a doctor, and after 40 minutes' flying he

Mildenhall-Melbourne Air Race in 1934 was won by C. W. A. Scott and T. Campbell Black, right, in a D.H. 88 Comet racer, *Grosvenor House*.   *The Aeroplane*

reached the place. But Elliott, who had been wounded in the arm by a bullet, died next day.

Yet another Elliott, again no relation to the author, lost his life in an accident involving one of Sir Alan Cobham's aircraft. He was ex-R.A.F. Sergeant Pilot William R. Elliott, who was educated at Pulham St. Mary Magdalene. Elliott, who was the chief flying instructor of the Irish Aero Club and an airman of considerable experience, was killed, and his passenger also, when his Gipsy Moth collided with a Fox Moth flown by ex-Flight Lieutenant Geoffrey Tyson, one of Sir Alan's pilots, at a display on July 7, 1933, at Limerick, Ireland. Elliott's machine fell a distance of 500 ft.

On October 20, 1934, Suffolk witnessed the start from Beck Row aerodrome, Mildenhall, of the Mildenhall-Melbourne Air Race, the greatest air race then or since. The race was for £15,000 and a £500 gold trophy offered by Sir MacPherson Robertson to commemorate the centenary of the city of Melbourne.

Mildenhall, it is interesting to remember, had been officially opened four days before—on October 16—and the aerodrome and hangars had been loaned to the Royal Aero Club for the occasion. No. 99 Squadron, equipped with Heyford bombers, did not in fact move in until November 15, 1934.

Sir Alan Cobham presented, in 1969, a trophy to R.A.F. Strike Command to be competed for annually by squadrons in the Command's Tanker Force. He is shown handing the Trophy to Air Marshal Sir Denis Spotswood at Marham.   *R.A.F. Marham*

The MacRobertson Race, as it was also called, was divided into two sections, a speed contest and a handicap race, both starting from Mildenhall. There were five compulsory stopping points between Mildenhall and Melbourne for entrants in the speed section—Baghdad, Allahabad, Singapore, Darwin and Charleville. All but two of the stage lengths between these places were over 2,000 miles long. In the handicap section, final places of entrants were determined by a formula.

The race, as can be imagined, attracted world wide attention, and a total of 64 entrants for both sections from the U.S.A., Britain, France, Holland, Australia, New Zealand, Italy, Sweden, Denmark, Germany, India, Eire, New Guinea and Portugal.

However, the total was considerably reduced, to 20, by withdrawals made either because the aeroplanes concerned did not conform to the contest's rules, or because of other circumstances, or because the aircraft could not arrive at Mildenhall before the latest time permitted by the Royal Aero Club regulations.

As the great day approached, (preparations started at Mildenhall a week before), the King and Queen and the Prince of Wales visited the aerodrome. With them was Lord Londonderry, the Air Minister. The county was strongly represented.

About this time there was a ceremony in the Royal Aero Club luncheon tent when Mrs. James A. Mollison, the late Miss Amy Johnson*, the intrepid woman aviator, who was to fly one of the D.H. 88 Comets with her husband, was handed a good luck mascot. Breaker of many flying records, James A. Mollison, who died in 1959 at the age of 54, took a short service commission in the R.A.F. and learnt to fly at the Flying Training School at Duxford, Cambridgeshire, in the early 1920s. When he took up flying at 18 he was the youngest officer in the Service.

It was a great day for philatelists and a post office was set up at Mildenhall aerodrome. Special covers were issued, some being signed by the pilots. But there was a more serious side to the post office. The officer in charge of the post office, a Mr. Bunett, was called upon to fulfill other tasks, including that of witnessing a number of wills.

Just after midnight on October 20, the race was to start at 6.30 a.m., hundreds of cars and thousands of people surrounded Mildenhall aerodrome. This was how the local press saw the scene at 4 a.m.: 'The roar of the aircraft engines, receiving their final ground tests, drowned all other sounds in the immediate vicinity, while the Comet to be flown by C. W. A. Scott and T. Campbell Black, the race favourites, was one of the machines spitting fierce flames . . .'.

Over at Newmarket big bets had already been laid on these two experienced airmen. Both Scott, the pilot, and Campbell Black, the co-pilot, were retired R.A.F. officers. Scott, who had West Mersea connections, one local newspaper described him as 'a burly East Anglian', was in all respects a most talented airmen.

*Amy Johnson died in the Thames on January 5, 1941, when the Airspeed Oxford she was piloting crashed for reasons unknown. The woman aviator's life has been well told by Constance Babington Smith in *Amy Johnson* (Collins) 1967.

Mr. Donald Parker, the brother of the late John Lankester Parker, the Suffolk aviator, whose early days have already been described, said of the Mildenhall-Melbourne air race: 'The occasion drew people from all over the country. Our house was full, with directors of Imperial Airways and of Short Bros; Oswald Short and my father got some clean straw and slept in the stable. Traffic was solid for miles around and some people, seeing the aerodrome lights in the near distance, left their cars, but unfortunately came to the River Lark'.

As zero hour came round, and a most beautiful autumn morning dawned over the fens, the great hangar doors at Mildenhall were rolled open to reveal, among other aircraft, Scott and Campbell Black's red Comet G-ACSS (No. 34) named 'Grosvenor House'*. About 70,000 spectators looked on, and 15,000 cars were parked in the area (some girls in tight fitting skirts even scaled the 60 ft. girders of a half finished hangar to get a better view).

Then, with a roar, the first team, the Mollisons, climbed away from Mildenhall on the greatest air race in history.

Scott noted: 'Low mists drifted beneath us as Mildenhall passed from sight, and once over the English coast-line we were swallowed in the haze of the North Sea'. The weather report for the Allahabad-Singapore run turned out to be as bad as the weather men had predicted. From his tiny cockpit Scott saw the heavens grow darker. He said: 'A great storm raged right and left of us, as clouds swept in battalions above, and still more ominous clouds rolled below. Steadily we flew on between them, with no chance of four hour shifts. Both of us were hard on the job, with feet on the rudder bar and hands on the control column'.

By the time Scott and Campbell Black landed at Singapore only the Dutchmen in a Douglas D.C. 2, a much larger aircraft, remained their challenging rivals. Then the leading Comet crew sped for Port Darwin across the inhospitable Timor Sea. What appeared to be a fault occurred in the port engine in darkness when they were still an hour from land. The oil pressure fell to zero. Mechanics at Port Darwin, however, could find no fault in the engine. It was, therefore, decided to race on to Charleville on what amounted to one engine. Subsequently a fault was found in the oil pressure gauge. Having taken on just enough fuel for the last lap, Scott and Campbell Black took the Comet off the ground at Charleville in the same uncertain state.

At 3.34 p.m. (local time) on October 23 the pair, physically and mentally exhausted, touched down the victors at Melbourne having covered 11,300 miles in 71 hours, 18 seconds at an average flying speed of 176.8 m.p.h. The *East Anglian Daily Times* on October 23, 1934, declared: 'Since Hawker and his companion flew upside down on the very first crossing of the Atlantic, no one can think of anything quite so fine'.

At West Mersea, where Scott was known, the old men of the sea talked into the night about the record. After all, in their young days, it used to take a sailing ship

*In Shuttleworth Collection.

at least 12 weeks to do the England-Australia run. The winning Comet, which is preserved today, was returned to England by boat in November, 1934. Its crew, too, came home by ship, it was the s.s. *Otranto* of the Orient Line, and a few years ago I was presented with a menu card issued on that voyage which bears the original signatures of Scott and Campbell Black: the latter, incidentally, lost his life in the Spanish Civil War. They took a month to return to England.

August 2-9, 1929, saw Captain C. D. Barnard, R. F. Little and the Duchess of Bedford embark on a flight from Croydon to Karachi, India. They flew there and back in a Fokker F.VII in fewer than eight days. Not long after this their Fokker, it bore the registration letters G-EBTS and was named 'The Spider', visited Norwich airport. The trio on April 10-19, 1930, flew from England to Cape Town in 10 days.

On March 22; 1937, the Duchess of Bedford, who was a skilled airwoman, came sharply into the news with East Anglia the centre of the drama. On that cold afternoon she took her tiny De Havilland Gypsy Moth biplane from the private airfield at Woburn, 15 miles from Bedford, and flew in the direction of the flooded Fens. She was then 71. And, what is more, she was in her 61st year when she flew solo for the first time and 68 when she got her pilot's licence. She regarded flying 'as the most exhilarating of sports'. It also eased the buzzing in her ears—she was very deaf—by changing the atmospheric pressure.

When the Duchess, clad in her usual leather coat, flying helmet and goggles, climbed away from Woburn that afternoon, her Gypsy Moth, with the registration letters G-ACUR, carried fuel for $3\frac{1}{2}$ hours if she needed to stay up that long.

Later that day, when she failed to return, great anxiety was felt for her safety.

Sir Alan Cobham's D.H. 61 Giant Moth G-AAEV, *Youth of Britain*, at Gorleston in 1929.   *C. R. Temple*

Left. Fokker F-VII *The Spider*, in which Capt. R. D. Barnard, R. F. Little and the Duchess of Bedford flew from Croydon to Karachi and back in 1929. Right. Duchess of Bedford who, at 71, was lost over Norfolk and coast.   *Peter Whymark*

The B.B.C. broadcast a message asking for clues. The R.A.F. was consulted and reported that, about the time of the Duchess's flight, a heavy snowstorm had occurred over Northamptonshire and Bedfordshire and that military aircraft had been forced to land in a hurry over a wide area. But it was true that, when the Duchess left Woburn, the weather in the area was favourable and some of East Anglia was free of cloud.

Many reports were received of her Gypsy Moth having been sighted. It seems likely that she headed for Bedford or Cambridge, then changed direction, possibly because of a build up of cloud to the west. Reports were received of an unidentified aircraft having passed over Holme-next-the-Sea, near Hunstanton, and out over the sea towards Boston. That was about 4.15 p.m. The Duchess had left Woburn at 3.30 p.m. But no one, at least at the time, could be certain that it was the missing Gypsy Moth.

By March 24 eight counties—Norfolk, Suffolk, Lincolnshire, Cambridgeshire, Bedfordshire, Huntingdonshire, Northamptonshire and Hertfordshire—had been searched on foot despite snow. The R.A.F.*, mindful of the Duchess's gallant contribution to British aviation, sent search aircraft from 10 aerodromes, including Mildenhall. Civilian aircraft, many flown by flying friends, also took the air. Lifeboats went out. Fishermen were asked to watch for aircraft wreckage. So were the coastguards. Beachcombers plodded the tide line at dawn seeking clues. All in all, the search must have been the biggest ever mounted in peace time in this country.

Then, on March 27, Flight Lieutenant R. C. Preston, the Duchess's personal pilot, sped from Woburn and 'established that a spar found at Sheringham was from the wing of a Moth aeroplane'. Fishermen who found it said that other wreckage was in the sea some way out. But still the evidence was not conclusive.

*For the devoted search undertaken by the R.A.F., which lasted eight days, the Duke of Bedford gave £1,000 to the R.A.F. Benevolent Fund.

Ten days after the Duchess disappeared a north east wind—the wind which brings amber and jet to the East Anglian beaches—drove an inter-plane strut ashore at Great Yarmouth. This time Flight Lieutenant Preston was able to confirm that it had come from the missing Gypsy Moth. The strut bore the letters D.H. (De Havilland) and, more important, on an aluminium bracket were the vital figures 41772 peculiar to that machine. About this time—April 2—three other similar struts came ashore at Gorleston, Lowestoft and Southwold. These struts, it seemed, had drifted from the direction of the Wash. The Great Yarmouth strut, for example, measured 4 ft. 8 in. by $4\frac{1}{2}$ in. A badly smashed propeller boss was washed up at Winterton.

So died the Duchess of Bedford who believed that one was never too old to learn to fly. But luck, on the whole, had been kind to her. Once nomadic Moors hit her aircraft with bullets. On the Karachi flight she and her crew had a narrow escape when the Fokker flew through a cluster of telephone wires at take off. Carbon-monoxide fumes nearly killed her on the Cape Town flight. And on another occasion, when fog blinded her over this country, she promptly took advantage of a space in Windsor Great Park! Thus, it seems, whatever led to her disappearance must have been beyond her airmanship, for did not the R.A.F. at the time report a snowstorm forcing down some of its own aircraft?

In 1964, when I was making inquiries about the disappearance of the Duchess of Bedford off the East Anglian coast, Mr. J. F. Fleming, of Hunstanton, reported that at the time of the Duchess's disappearance he was building a riding school at Holme-next-Sea. 'It was a clear day', he said, 'and late in the afternoon I drew the attention of

The late Sir Raymond Quilter carried out many parachute descents including several delayed free falls.
Lady Margery Quilter

one of the grooms to an aeroplane which passed along the Wash with its engine stalling and spluttering . . . I have a vivid recollection that the colour of the plane was light blue'. Mr. Hubert Groom, of Wells, disclosed that the Duchess had asked permission to land on a 50 acre field he had at Warham which was very level and had no pot holes. She used it several times. He added: 'No doubt she was looking for it when she crashed within a mile of it just off Stiffkey. My shepherd had his lambing yard quite near the sea and heard the explosion out to sea . . . I think we must conclude that this was where the Duchess ended her life . . .'.

When Sir Raymond Quilter*, the son of Sir Cuthbert Quilter, second baronet, of Methersgate Hall, Woodbridge, died in 1959 it was the passing of one of the country's leading parachute experts, his interest in the manufacture and improvement of parachutes going back 30 years. He made many descents, including several delayed free falls. Sir Raymond was well known as an amateur airman, and flew his own aircraft, which he once described as 'the best radio-equipped private aircraft in Britain', from a private airfield on his estate in Suffolk. His grandfather, Sir Cuthbert Quilter, first baronet, built Bawdsey Manor which was taken over in the 1930s as Britain's first radar laboratory.

Col. Roscoe Turner, who came third in the Mildenhall-Melbourne Air Race, carried this cover in the mail aboard his Boeing 247 D. *Author*

*A little known activity of Sir Raymond's in 1939-1945—it was a hobby with him—was bomb disposal. In this connection he produced a useful tool called the 'Quilter key' for extracting fuses from enemy bombs.

CHAPTER XII

Preparations for Total War

IN THE January, 1934, edition of *Popular Flying,* the late W. E. Johns, Editor, wrote an article entitled 'Where Stands Germany?'. He said: 'In the matter of personnel, Germany is a nation of flyers. Flying has become a national sport. Aviation meetings are attended by vast crowds. Even a gliding meeting is attended by everyone, young and old alike, within reach'.

What answer did we have to the growing might? Well, in July, 1934, the British government initiated the R.A.F. Expansion Scheme. Public announcement of the expansion was made in May, 1935. By April, 1936, 32 new stations, several in East Anglia, had been or were being built or acquired.

When W. E. Johns wrote of Germany's growing aerial might the R.A.F. could then muster 850 first line aircraft, of which the fastest was the 207 m.p.h. Hawker Fury biplane fighter, and the most potent bomber was the lumbering Handley Page Heyford with a range of 500 miles and bomb load of 3,000 lb. The year 1934 also saw the start of Empire Air Day displays—another move to get the British air minded.

In 1935, the day was Saturday, July 6, Mildenhall, which a few years later was to become the heart of Bomber Command's early activities, saw the cream of the R.A.F. reviewed in honour of King George V's silver jubilee. Nearly 40 squadrons, about 400 officers and nearly 4,000 men, assembled at this famous airfield, where the King, as Chief of the R.A.F., accompanied by the Prince of Wales and the Duke of York, saw 350 aircraft—Heyfords, Fairey Hendons, Gloster Gauntlets, Hawker Harts, Hawker Demons, Hawker Furies, Bristol Bulldogs and so on—drawn up in a great arc. He was received by the Lord Lieutenant of Suffolk, Sir Courtenay Warner, who was dressed in cocked hat and uniform of black and silver.

After the inspection at Mildenhall, the royal party, incidentally, travelled a distance of some five miles in motor cars to inspect the eight lines of aircraft, the royal visitors went to Duxford, via beflagged Worlington and Newmarket, where the Queen and the Duchess of York joined them at luncheon in the officers' mess before the fly past.

Altogether 20 of the 38 squadrons at Mildenhall took off, and following carefully arranged smoke signals from the ground, the very mixed formations, led by No. 99 Squadron, made up of 182 machines, without a single engine fault, bore down on the Duxford royal dais like a cloud out of an empty sky.

After the review the King sent the following message to the Secretary of State for Air (Sir Philip Cunliffe-Lister): 'I warmly congratulate all ranks of the R.A.F. . . . I was greatly impressed both by their smartness on the ground and their efficiency in the air, which leave no doubt that they will prove fully equal to any task which they may be called upon to fulfil. . .'.

The Times for July 8 added: 'No better display has ever been made before a ruler and perhaps no king could more fully appreciate its significance than King George who saw the same Force on active service in the days of his youth'.

As the R.A.F. expanded new aircraft were introduced. For example, when the royal inspection took place in East Anglia in 1935, King George was able to see the Gloster Gauntlet biplane, first of the new fighters, in the hands of No. 19 Squadron at Duxford. At that time the prototypes of the Hurricane and Spitfire, the first Spitfires went to 19 Squadron in August, 1938, had already flown. Although there were a few monoplanes in service with the R.F.C. and the R.A.F. World War I, 1936 marked the beginning of the real changeover from biplane to monoplane. November, 1936, saw the R.A.F.'s first all metal low wing cantilever monoplane, the Fairey Hendon, enter service, the first joining No. 38 Squadron at Mildenhall. The Hendon, powered by two 600 h.p. Rolls-Royce Kestrel engines, had a crew of five, flew at 155 m.p.h. at 15,000 ft. and carried a bomb load of 1,660 lb.

In 1935, as already related, Mildenhall was the scene of one of the grandest inspections in the history of the R.A.F. Then, in October, 1937, it received a top level German Air Force mission consisting of General Hans-Juergen Stumpff, Feldmarschall Erhard Milch, General Ernst Udet, General Wenniger, the German Air Attache in London, and Majors Nielsen and Kreipe. The mission travelled from London by rail on October 19 and were met by car at Cambridge, arriving at Mildenhall at 11.45 a.m. They were received at the R.A.F. station by the Air Officer Commanding, Bomber Command, Air Chief Marshal Sir Edgar R. Ludlow-Hewitt, and walked between two rows of Handley Page Heyford bombers from Nos. 99 and 149 Squadrons. Subsequently the party inspected certain types of aircraft—Handley Page Harrow, Armstrong Whitworth Whitley, Vickers Wellesley and Bristol Blenheim—and certain items of technical equipment. There was a fly past of new and medium and heavy bombers, and by the early afternoon the German delegation must have been well pleased with the intelligence they had been given on a plate. General Milch, a large man, sat down with his colleagues for lunch in the officers' mess, that was at 1 o'clock, and at 3 o'clock the German party left by air for the R.A.F. College at Cranwell, Lincolnshire, where they stayed the night.

We have already touched on the research and development work which was undertaken at Felixstowe and Martlesham Heath. In the mid-1930s, when farsighted Englishmen were feeling uneasy about Germany's growing military strength, some of the best scientific brains in the country set to work to develop radar. It was, in fact, from Orfordness, on the Suffolk coast, that the research team moved to Bawdsey Manor on the River Deben estuary.

Bawdsey Manor purchased as a research centre for radar from the Quilter family in 1935.

Lady Margery Quilter

When in early 1968 Government secret papers for the period 1922 to 1937 were made available for the first time at the Public Record Office, London, it became clear that between 1928 and 1931, and before Hitler came to power, Britain and Germany co-operated in the development of equipment for detecting thunderstorms—the very aspect of detection which gave the R.A.F. its 'eyes' in the Battle of Britain in 1940. Germany furthermore provided the funds for this research, and a file on the Radio Research Board records this fact.

Mr. Robert Watson-Watt, the radar pioneer, who was later knighted, had brought back from Germany a cathode ray oscillograph which was used for making visible, electrical signals. The cathode ray direction finder, when set up, was used for picking up signals from atmospheric radio disturbances such as thunderstorms. These signals were recorded as 'blips', the forerunners of the signals on the earliest radar sets.

Orfordness was known to the scientists as 'The Island', made so by the rivers Ore and Alde on one side and the sea on the other. Orfordness had been used for armament research for many years when the scientists arrived in 1935. The Crown and Castle Hotel, Orford, which was reached by crossing the river, was a favourite meeting place for the scientists, and it is said that the sitting room at the hotel became an unofficial conference room for evening talks.

On September 16, 1935, Bawdsey Manor was purchased from Sir Cuthbert Quilter* so that the early work at Orfordness, which had proved so promising, could be pursued in bigger laboratories. Apparently the north end of the Manor's sea front, with its 70

*The first Sir Cuthbert Quilter, the builder of the so-called Bawdsey Manor, started to build the 'huge pile' in 1886 and apparently continued the pastime for 20 years. Allan Jobson, writing about old Bawdsey in the *Mercury Series* for July 28, 1967, commented: 'His original idea was a seaside home costing about £4,000 but the craze to keep up the momentum created what his successors must have realised was a white elephant'. But was it such a white elephant in the light of later events?

ft. elevation, attracted the scientists. The stables and outbuildings of the Manor were converted into laboratories. A great reward was in store for the clever brains of Bawdsey Manor, for the practical application of their work was one of the key reasons why the Battle of Britain was won.

In *The Narrow Margin,* the definitive story of the Battle of Britain, Derek Wood with Derek Dempster noted: 'On July 24, 1935, while awaiting the return of a Westland Wallace biplane which was followed out to 34 miles, a new echo was observed at 20 miles. From its fluctuations the ground operators inferred that the echo consisted of three aircraft. For the first time radar had identified a formation. The pilot of the Wallace confirmed that it consisted of three Hawker Hart bombers which flew on blissfully unaware that their passage had been observed by the small group in the hut at Orfordness'.

Squadron Leader (later Air Marshal Sir) Raymond Hart was posted to Bawdsey in July, 1936, as the first R.A.F. officer on the staff. His main task was to organise a school for radar training, and in February, 1937, the first radar training school in the world was officially opened.

In June, 1937, Bawdsey was, at that time, the only completed station in the proposed radar chain which was to protect the British Isles from the Tyne to Southampton. Apart from Bawdsey, other East Anglian radar stations of the war years existed at High Street, Darsham; at Stoke Holy Cross, near Norwich and at West Beckham, near Holt, guarding the Wash area. Stoke Holy Cross was not apparently a success.

Prime Minister Winston Churchill, in Vol. 1 of *The Second World War,* said that on June 20, 1939, Sir Henry Tizard, Rector of the Imperial College of Science and Technology, 'conducted me in a rather disreputable aeroplane to see the establishments which had been developed on the East Coast . . .'.

Of Mr. Churchill's visit to Bawdsey Manor in 1939, Sir Robert Watson-Watt, in *Three Steps to Victory,* said: 'We did our tricks for him, and foolishly tried to explain to him what was inside some of our black boxes'.

Not long before this visit the German 'Graf Zeppelin' airship flew up the East Coast of Britain in an endeavour, so the history books say, to find out what we were putting out in the way of radio pulses and the like. The airship paid attention to Bawdsey Manor and Orfordness. Mr. Churchill, in Vol. 1, threw some light on this strange flight: 'General Wolfgang Martini, Director-General of Signals in the Luftwaffe, had arranged that she carried special listening equipment to discover the existence of British radar transmissions, if any. The attempt failed, but had her listening equipment been working properly the "Graf Zeppelin" ought certainly to have been able to carry back to Germany the information that we had radar, for our radar stations were not only operating at the time, but also detected her movements and divined her intention . . .'.

1) Sir Robert Watson-Watt.

2) Original filter table map at Bawdsey in 1938.

3) First large formation seen on the Bawdsey cathode ray tube in 1938.

4) Radar Station at Darsham opened late 1930s, demolished 1957.

SUFFOLK AND RADAR

Derek Wood and Author

One-armed Charles Robert Brinkley, who used to be the ferryman at Felixstowe Ferry and knew many of the Bawdsey Manor scientists, has left his name in the pages of history. For when a handy copper hoop used in the laboratories was appropriately named 'The Brinkley', after the ferryman's hooked arm, he was blown up by a faulty muzzle-loader in the 1890s, a development engineer used the term in written R.A.F. instructions—and to this day the description is in the records.

In the course of visiting many sites of interest in connection with the growth of aviation in East Anglia, I never got very close to any of the early radar sites, but I remember being taken near the Bawdsey site before 1939. In letters I wrote at the time, I was 10, I reiterated the rumour, then very strong in Suffolk, that the Suffolk masts were for a secret ray which would stop engines.

Wattisham airfield, near Ipswich, which was to see so much action in the 1939-1945 war, was opened in April, 1939, and in May two Blenheim bomber squadrons, Nos. 107 and 110, which later that year made the first bombing attack of the war, moved in. From the opening to April, 1941, the station was commanded by Group Captain (later Air Commodore) Oswald R. Gayford*, who lived for many years at Naughton and died in August, 1945. Gayford House, the station commander's residence, is named after him at Wattisham.

Air Commodore Gayford, whose name is commemorated on a plaque in St. Mary's Church, Naughton, was an exponent of long distance flying. On October 27/28, 1931, he flew a Fairey (Napier) Long Range Monoplane from Cranwell, in Lincolnshire, to Abu Sueir, Egypt, non-stop in $31\frac{1}{2}$ hours. His navigator was Flight-Lieutenant D. L. G. Betts. On February 6/8, 1933, the then Squadron Leader Gayford, with Flight Lieutenant G. E. (later Air Marshal Sir Gilbert) Nicholetts as navigator, set up a world's distance record of 5,309 miles, also in a Fairey Long Range Monoplane. They flew to Walvis Bay, South Africa, in 52 hours 25 minutes. A little more than five years later Vickers Wellesley single-engined bombers belonging to the R.A.F. Long Range Development Flight, which had been formed under the then Wing Commander Gayford, established the world's distance record, two of them flying 7,162 miles non-stop from Ismailia, Egypt, to Darwin, Australia. The record was then held by the U.S.S.R. at 6,306 miles. The capture of the record by the R.A.F. won for the Service the Britannia Challenge Trophy, presented by the Royal Aero Club, for the most meritorious performance of the year by British airmen.

The 1939 edition of the *Suffolk County Handbook and Official Directory* gave information about the composition of the R.A.F. in the county as war approached. Mildenhall was the headquarters of No. 3 Bomber Group. Two bomber squadrons—Nos. 99 and 149—were stationed there. At Honington, near Bury St. Edmunds, Nos. 75 and 215 were in position. Over at Stradishall, near Newmarket, two more squadrons waited—Nos. 9 and 148. But as war drew nearer the East Anglian based squadrons

*Awards: C.B.E., D.F.C., A.F.C.

started to change aerodromes and learn dispersal. September, 1939, was to see six squadrons of No. 2 Bomber Group in East Anglia with Blenheim IV bombers, and six squadrons of No. 3 Bomber Group, also in Eastern England, equipped with Wellington I and IA bombers.

Whilst war clouds had gathered as the 1939 edition of the Suffolk Directory went to press few anticipated that the storm would break so soon. On September 3, 1939 war was declared and, although the year had yet months to run, an era in the chronicles of man's endeavours in the air over East Anglia had come to an end.

Spitfires of 19 Squadron at Duxford in 1938. *Vickers Ltd.*

Bibliography

Among the books and periodicals consulted were:

The History of Aeronautics in Great Britain (J. E. Hodgson). Oxford University Press 1924.

Wonders of World Aviation (edited by Clarence Winchester). The Waverley Book Co. 1938.

Norwich (general editor Major E. Felce). A. E. Soman 1935.

The Crowded Sky (edited by Neville Duke and Edward Lanchbery). Cassell 1959.

The British Rigid Airship 1908-1931 (Robin Higham). G. T. Foulis 1961.

R.A.F. Badges (issued by John Player & Sons). Imperial Tobacco Co. 1937.

The Old Flying Days (Major C. C. Turner). Sampson Low, Marston 1927.

A History of Jesus College Cambridge (Arthur Gray and Frederick Brittain). Heinemann 1960.

The Flying Cathedral (Arthur Gould Lee). Methuen 1965.

Trenchard (Andrew Boyle). Collins 1962.

A Short Record of the East Anglian Munitions Committee in the Great War 1914-1918 (Sir Wilfrid Stokes). Silk & Terry 1919.

The German Air Raids on Great Britain 1914-1918 (Captain Joseph Morris). Sampson Low, Marston 1925.

Report on Police Observation Work in connection with Raids by Hostile Aircraft and Men-of-War on the County of East Suffolk (Assistant Chief Constable G. S. Staunton). W. S. Cowell 1919.

The Defence of London (A. Rawlinson). Andrew Melrose 1923.

Pigeons in the Great War (Lt.-Col. A. H. Osman). The Racing Pigeon Publishing Co. 1919.

The British Fighter Since 1912 (Peter Lewis). Putnam 1965.

The Prof In Two Worlds (F. W. F. Smith). Collins 1961.

Testing Time: A Study of Man and Machine in the Test Flying Era (Constance Babington Smith). Cassell 1961.

Flying Boat: The Story of the Sunderland (Kenneth Poolman). William Kimber 1962.

No Parachute: A Fighter Pilot in World War I (Arthur Gould Lee). Jarrolds 1968.

The Story of a North Sea Air Station (C. F. Snowden Gamble). Oxford University Press 1928.

Three Steps to Victory (Sir Robert Watson-Watt). Odhams 1957.

From Sea To Sky (Air Marshal Sir Arthur Longmore). Geoffrey Bles 1946.

Pioneer Aircraft 1903-1914 (Kenneth Munson). Blandford Press 1969.

Sky-Riders (foreword by Alex. Henshaw). Collins 1936.

Complete Book of Aviation (C. G. Burge). Pitman 1935.

The Aeronauts: A History of Ballooning 1783-1903 (L. T. C. Rolt). Longman, Green & Co. 1966.

R.A.F. 1939-1945: *The Fight At Odds*, Vol. 1 (Denis Richards). H.M.S.O. 1953.

The Second World War: The Gathering Storm, Vol. 1 (Winston S. Churchill). Cassell 1948.

R.A.F. Official Programme: Empire Air Day Martlesham Heath, 1938 (The Air League of the British Empire).

The Illustrated London News Silver Jubilee Record Number 1910-1935 (seven authors).

Slide Rule (Nevil Shute). Heinemann 1954.

Winston S. Churchill, Companion Vol. II. Part 3, 1911-1914 (Randolph Churchill). Heinemann 1969.

Women With Wings (Pauline Gower). John Long 1938.

Selected Letters of T. E. Lawrence (Edited by David Garnett). Jonathan Cape 1952.

Experiments on Rigid Airship R.33 (J. R. Pannell and R. A. Frazer). H.M.S.O. 1921.

Suffolk County Handbook and Official Directory 1939 (East Anglian Daily Times).

Boulton And Paul In The Great War (Henry ffiske): *The House of Boulton and Paul Ltd.*: *Air Ministry News Letter* (various issues): *Air Pictorial*: *Flight* (now *Flight International*): *Air-Britain Digest*.

The Life-boat: *East Anglian Magazine*: *Eastern Daily Press*: *East Anglian Daily Times*: *Suffolk Mercury Series*: *Norwich Mercury Series*: *Shell Aviation News*: *War Pictorial*: *Straightaway*: *Pulham Patrol*: *The Wing*.

Sotheby & Co. (sale of aeronautical prints and drawings March 20, 1962).

INDEX